Radical Bowhunter

Matt
" Be Radical"
Nick
Scamfu

RADICAL BOWHUNTER

Serious Tactics for Taking Trophy Whitetails

Dick Scorzafava

STACKPOLE
BOOKS

Published by
STACKPOLE BOOKS
5067 Ritter Road
Mechanicsburg, PA 17055
www.stackpolebooks.com

Printed in the United States

10 9 8 7 6 5 4 3 2

First edition

Photographs by the author except where noted
Illustrations by Kerry Handel
Cover design by Wendy A. Reynolds
Cover photograph by John Dziza

Library of Congress Cataloging-in-Publication Data

Scorzafava, Dick.
  Radical bowhunter : serious tactics for taking trophy whitetails / Dick Scorzafava.— 1st ed.
    p. cm.
  Includes index.
  ISBN-13: 978-0-8117-3307-6
  ISBN-10: 0-8117-3307-6
  1. White-tailed deer hunting. 2. Bowhunting. I. Title.

SK301.S27 2006
799.2'7652—dc22
                                                    2005027260

Contents

Foreword

A number of years ago, I decided to write an article based on interviews of several bowhunters who seemed to always get their big bucks. My goal was to determine the commonalities among all of these hunters' methods, to unlock their secrets of bagging bucks. When all was said and done, the only commonality I found was that all of these profoundly successful bowhunters had developed their own unique way of consistently filling their tag. What each of them did was different from the others and certainly different from how I hunted.

Since writing that article, whenever I have the opportunity, I grill successful bowhunters to learn their particular "secrets." One such victim has been Dick Scorzafava, a pro staffer for many companies I am affiliated with who has become a good friend. During one particular bowhunting season, both Dick and I both drew tags to hunt Iowa. We'd frequently compare notes, but it wasn't until the end of the season that I figured out why Dick bagged his trophy and I did not.

It seemed like Dick has traveled back and forth between his home state of Massachusetts and Iowa numerous times. I finally asked him how many days he'd hunted that particular big deer. After counting, Dick told me he had hunted twenty-three days. I counted. I had hunted six and a half days. My first reaction was one of vindication. I told Dick that surely I, too, could have bagged the big buck I was after if I had twenty-three days to hunt in Iowa.

After further thought, a light bulb went on, and I realized I had discovered yet another difference between a consistently successful hunter such as Dick and a weekend warrior like me. Dick Scorzafava is a humble man. He does not like to toot his own horn, so I will. Few of the biggest names in bowhunting have as many record-book bucks as Dick. And few have as many true monsters. Why? Well that's what this book is about. Dick does what it takes. He thinks outside the proverbial box. He is not a radical man, but he is a radical bowhunter.

Like the saying goes, "continue to think the way you've always thought and continue to get what you've always got." Dick Scorzafava, the radical bowhunter, will change the way you hunt.

Walt Larsen
President, Scales Outdoor Group

P.S. If you look at the number on the back of Dick's Mathews trading card you'll see it is card 23. This is in honor of the number of days it took Dick to bag that Iowa buck.

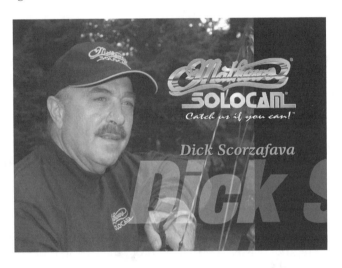

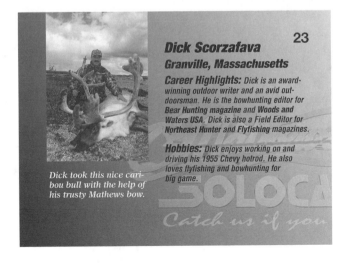

Acknowledgments

This book would not have been possible without the help of dozens of dedicated family members and close friends. These people share my passion that the information in this book will help you create opportunities for bowhunting the trophy whitetail buck of your dreams. I hope that by sharing my knowledge, it may change your life for the better. Everyone who reads these pages can, given the proper mindset and effort, become a radical bowhunter and a responsible member of the hunting community.

It is almost impossible to identify every person, manufacturer, or organization that in some way helped me in the creation of this book. No doubt I will miss someone in my efforts to name as many as possible. If so, please forgive me and know that your contribution was nonetheless much appreciated.

I am deeply grateful to Jimmy McDonough, game biologist and deer project leader, whose loving guidance, skill, patience, and tireless efforts over the years developed me into the radical bowhunter I am today. This wonderful man was never too busy for me or above sharing his knowledge with me even when I was just a young kid. That says something about Jim McDonough as a man. I am fortunate to call him my friend.

My heartfelt thanks to Frank Sousa, who pushed me to write a bowhunting column for his magazine many years ago, which launched my writing career, and to my photographer buddy John Dziza, for all the exceptional photos he has taken for me over the years, many of which you'll enjoy throughout this book. I also appreciate Walt Larsen, whose support, guidance, and friendship over the last several years has fine-tuned my writing and marketing skills in the industry. Walt gave me a hard shove to see this book grow beyond the dream stage into a reality. Thanks, pal.

Thanks also to the people who were particularly helpful and supportive in the research of this project because of our true friendships: Greg Sesslemann and George Schrink of Scent-Lok Technologies; Ron Bice of Wildlife Research Center; Matt McPherson, Joel Maxfield, and Mike Ziebell of Mathews Inc.; Mark Cuddeback of Non Typical Inc.; Dave Larsen of Gamehide; Steve Scott of the Whitetail Institute; Mike Ellig of Montana Black Gold; Larry Pulkrabek of Field Logic; Brooks Johnson and Keith Beam of Double Bull Blinds; Preston Pittman, owner of Pittman Game Calls; Deb Lazenby of Thorlo; Greg Hood, owner of Southern Game Calls; Rory Bower of Deerview Inc.; and Pat Gorman of Integrated Safety.

Last but not least I want to thank all the friends and family who have supported me through the many years of bowhunting, bowhunting, and more bowhunting; during the many missed Thanksgiving dinners; and finally while writing this book.

Introduction

Who or what is the radical bowhunter? The answer involves more of a state of mind than an actual personality type, although that certainly comes into play. I have an A-type personality and am in a constant state of motion from morning to night. I have lists, my lists have lists, and sometimes I even manage to leave my wife a list—while I'm off hunting, of course. Now is that radical?

This book is not for the person who goes hunting one week during the year as a vacation or bonding ritual with five or six buddies. There is nothing wrong with that, but this book is aimed at the person who has more of a commitment to the sport than an annual weekend hunting-lodge getaway.

I hunt every day, 365 days a year. Not all of this hunting is done in the woods. Most of it is done during the off-season, in the comfort of my easy chair. Not a day goes by that I don't spend some time thinking about bowhunting. I may read a book, write an article, research a topic or potential hot spot, practice with my newest bow, make plans to hunt, or simply relive a hunt. But truth be told, thoughts of bowhunting occupy part of every day.

This is the type of commitment I have to being a serious bowhunter, a radical bowhunter.

Does this mean that you must go to my extremes to become a radical bowhunter? No. But what it does mean is that you must put forth effort in many different areas to learn the skills and tactics necessary to realize your full potential at bagging monster bucks. By becoming a radical bowhunter, you will ascend to a higher level than the casual hunter or even the meat hunter. You will join an elite group who bring the hunt to a new level of challenge, where you pursue a specific buck, not merely any buck; go one-on-one with one of the most magnificent and majestic creatures of North America; and have as your goal to emerge as the victor in the age-old contest between the bowhunter for dominance and the buck for survival.

PART ONE

WHERE:

If you want to bag a big buck, you must first find a big buck

CHAPTER 1

All Areas Are Not Created Equal

Whether or not you consider yourself to be a radical bowhunter, or one in the making, one thing is sure: If you cannot find a big buck, then there is no way you can get one in your sights and ultimately have a trophy hanging on your wall. It sounds so simple, so obvious. But let me assure you that many hunters who leave the warmth of their beds and the comforts of home in pursuit of this thing called a trophy haven't a clue where to find one. They may know where to find white-tailed deer in general, but if they have not stepped up the competition to one-on-one, then they are not yet radical bowhunters. It doesn't mean that they are not very successful hunters; it merely means that they have not yet become discriminating. They have not yet gotten to the point where just any deer will not do.

In order to become a radical bowhunter, you need to step up the competition to the next level, to pursue a specific buck that will test all of your skills, put all of your knowledge to use, and drive you crazy in the bargain. To meet on this field of battle, you must hunt in a location that is populated with superbucks, or else the deck is already stacked overwhelmingly against you.

Over the past couple decades, the total white-tailed deer population, as well as their range, has expanded to the point that many biologists and game managers are working to stabilize or even reduce the herds in the areas under their control. This has greatly increased the interest in trophy whitetail hunting and record-book entries across the animal's North American range. In fact, more than 50 percent of the total record-book bucks entered have been harvested since 1990.

A majority of record-book bucks come from a handful of locations—places like Allamakee County, Iowa; Buffalo County, Wisconsin; Pike County, Illinois; the state of Kansas; and the Canadian province of

Saskatchewan find their way into the entries time and time again. Twenty-eight of the top fifty trophy-producing areas across the whitetail's North American range are counties in Iowa and Illinois, making these states great trophy hot spots for bowhunters. The radical bowhunter will capitalize on this information, and these spots will become nirvana to him. The radical bowhunter will flinch when his wife mentions a Caribbean cruise but salivate when he hears mention of any of these places. I have no idea why a self-respecting trophy buck would want to hail from a place called Buffalo County, but they are there, take my word for it.

How many articles or books have you read over the years telling you where to hunt that monster buck of which dreams are made? The problem with most of these articles is that they are general and very vague. Realizing this shortfall, I'm going to give you all the meat and potatoes you can swallow. Better yet, the information will be backed up with hard facts.

I firmly believe that the heyday of trophy white-tailed deer hunting is right now, and your success can continue to increase if you are hunting the proper locations. Back in the early 1900s, spotting a white-tailed deer was a rarity in many states and provinces. In many areas, they had become almost totally extinct. Factors such as unrestricted market hunting, deforestation, and conversion of land to agriculture were some of the major reasons for the species' decline in numbers.

Where there were vast areas of agriculture and the land had been cleared, the deer were especially vulnerable because they had nowhere to hide. In many of these areas, the herds did not return to numbers where a modern hunting season was possible until the 1940s and 1950s. On the other hand, in regions that were forested and remote, such as Maine, South Texas, Wisconsin, and the Mississippi Delta, white-tailed deer were able to survive in much greater numbers because these wooded areas provided safe habitat. Places like Buffalo County, Wisconsin, became deer havens. One reason this area is so fertile today, and has become one of the all-time best trophy-producing areas in North America, is that it was not glaciated during the last ice age. The topography was not scraped flat and bare by the glacial ice sheet. The rugged hills and valleys are difficult to farm, except for the occasional flat spot, so a lot of forest cover remains. Buffalo County's landscape of forested hills provides abundant food and cover for deer not only to survive, but also to grow—and grow big.

Why some areas consistently produce more trophies than others is a difficult question to answer. Many factors, both human and natural, must be considered. But one tenet that often comes to the forefront is the relationship between river systems and the number of trophy bucks in an area. This underlying component is evident across the entire range of the white-tailed deer. If you analyze the top trophy buck counties across the country, the pattern stands out clearly—big rivers mean big deer. It is especially evident in counties with river bottoms along the Missouri, Mississippi, and Ohio Rivers, which run through the center of the country.

Still another pattern is that the areas with higher deer densities, long and liberal gun seasons, and multiple tags habitually produce substantially fewer trophy bucks than areas with much lower densities of whitetails, shorter firearms seasons, and limits of only one deer tag per season. A state's management practices can have a dramatic impact on the number of potential trophies a given area can produce. In my home state of Massachusetts, as well as in Iowa, the modern gun and muzzleloader seasons open after the rut is over, which means less buck movement as the breeding cycle is winding down. Less pressure and fewer deer moving means fewer deer for hunters to bag, which gives these surviving deer a chance to mature and become trophy-class bucks. The muzzleloader

Greg Sesselmann, president of Scent-Lok Technologies, with an impressive Kansas buck.

A magnificent trophy harvested by George Shrink, vice president of Scent-Lok.

season in Kansas falls in the middle of September, when the trees still provide lots of cover. The daily temperatures can be much warmer, causing the deer to stay bedded down to avoid the heat. These things can make it harder for hunters to locate good bucks, resulting in more bucks living longer and thus becoming trophies.

In Missouri, the rifle season usually opens up right at the beginning of the peak of the rut, bringing man and deer into contact as each are on a quest, the buck for a hot doe, the hunter for that buck. In Oklahoma, the muzzleloader season usually opens sometime in mid to late October and runs into November, when bucks are starting to chase does in the rut and the daily temperatures are much cooler. These management practices mean that more mature bucks are bagged during hunting seasons, leaving fewer bucks to have the extra seasons needed to develop into trophy-class animals.

Dick's "border buck," a heavily racked ten-pointer taken in Missouri, just over the Iowa line. Notice the sticker points.

Analyzing the hunting seasons' timetables shows that most monster bucks are taken during the firearms seasons, so their timing is critical. Seasons that fall before or after the rut, when bucks are much less vulnerable, give the bucks in the herd the time they need to mature into trophy animals.

I learned at an early age, when I was doing whitetail studies with our state deer biologist Jim McDonough, who was my mentor, that all areas are not created equal. Some areas of a given state or province always produce more deer than others. And a few areas seem to produce the really big trophy bucks year in and year out. That is true across the entire North American range of the white-tailed deer.

If you want to kill a trophy-class buck, and do so consistently, there is a simple solution: You have to hunt where these big bucks exist in decent numbers so you will have a realistic opportunity at bagging that buck of

These big Massachusetts beauties were harvested on both public and private land. Each scored over 140.

your dreams. It stands to reason that your best bet to harvest a trophy buck is to hunt where the odds statistically are in your favor.

There are still places where the bowhunter has a great chance of releasing an arrow at a world-class whitetail. Close your eyes and dream of giant-bodied bucks with long, heavy tines and sprawling racks. Fair-chase hunts exist in places that give you plenty of elbow room to set up and hunt with your bow. All it takes to find one of these places is to do some serious homework. One word of caution, though: Never get complacent about the hot spot you eventually find. Continually search out new and better locations to hunt. Once several trophy-class animals have been taken from a locality, ripples of excitement spread throughout the bowhunting community, and it doesn't take long after word gets out for an area to start declining in trophy potential as more and more hunters invade the spot to try their luck. Over the years, I have never seen an area get better over time in such situations. The trophy harvest always declines as hunting pressure increases.

On the Internet, the data available for bowhunters increases daily. Many national and regional organizations have record books and interactive websites with up-to-date information. On the national level, Boone and Crockett, Pope and Young, and the Quality Deer Management Association (QDMA) have outstanding websites that will help you find trophy hot spots to hunt. They also offer quarterly publications packed with useful statistics.

Top Ten Trophy Hot Spots in North America (*In Alphabetical Order*)	
Allamakee County, Iowa	Pike County, Illinois
Buffalo County, Wisconsin	Ringgold County, Iowa
Carroll County, Illinois	Sweet Grass, Saskatchewan, Canada
Hopkins County, Kentucky	St. Louis County, Minnesota
Nemaha County, Kansas	Swan River, Manitoba, Canada

Ten states or provinces account for slightly more than 70 percent of the total trophy white-tailed deer entries into the Boone and Crockett's all-time record book. This may be hard to fathom—until you analyze the information in the B&C book. This is the kind of useful information that can get you started in narrowing down your search for where you should set up your treestands or blind this fall in pursuit of a trophy buck.

In addition to destination information, the websites provide interesting facts, such as what measurements are most important when field-judging a whitetail buck and how to score bucks with big eight-point racks, because the Boone and Crockett and Pope and Young scoring systems are designed for ten-point frames. There is no end to the quality information that you can access on these websites. To become a radical bowhunter, forget the chat rooms. You need facts, not idle conversation and hearsay. Your computer can be a great asset in doing research if you spend time in the right places.

Many state fish and wildlife agencies provide statistical data on their websites and in record books as well. For example, the top ten counties in terms of the number of bucks recorded in the Iowa Big Game Records are displayed on a map of the state. Kansas lists the top twenty typical and nontypical bucks taken in the state, broken down by county and method of harvest: archery, muzzleloader, or modern rifle. The Northeast Big Buck Club (NEBBC) is an extremely useful reference source for the entire northeastern region of the country.

Most of these websites are well maintained and constantly updated. They provide outstanding, timely material that will help in your pursuit of that trophy buck of your dreams. It doesn't take a rocket scientist to figure out that if you want to kill big bucks you must hunt where big bucks exist. These tools—either online or in book form—can be invaluable sources for the trophy hunter to research and analyze. They can help put you where you can make your dreams reality. An old saw states that a workman is only as good as his tools; well, here are some pretty powerful tools. All you have to do is use them. If you want to become a radical bowhunter, you'll have to become a good researcher and somewhat of a statistician—not necessarily able to spew out facts and figures, but capable of gathering and analyzing the data in preparation for a dream hunt that will land you a monster buck.

CHAPTER 2

Build a Big-Buck Factory

With proper nutrition and management, big bucks can be grown just about anywhere. Depending on the availability of whitetail habitat, you may decide to take a radical step and build your own big-buck factory, providing an environment that will foster the growth of large-bodied and heavy-antlered whitetail bucks. What better way to find and harvest a beauty of a wall-hanger than by structuring an optimal environment in which they can thrive? This is a long-term project, but many hunting clubs and even individuals are creating or enhancing hunting grounds so that they may yield healthier and larger deer with superior racks that will score higher than those of native deer left to their own devices and the whims of Mother Nature. Creating a habitat conducive to whitetail bucks, with a highly nutritional food source in the form of a food plot supplemented with much-needed vitamins and minerals, will provide deer with a banquet of browse and fodder and keep bucks within your hunting area.

NUTRITION AND DEER GROWTH

Perhaps the best indicator of range quality is the physical size of young male deer. The better nutrition a white-tailed deer receives, the healthier, heavier, and larger it will be at maturity. One of the most obvious results is antler growth. But just as with humans, proper nutrition will affect many other aspects of the deer's overall health.

Research programs, such as those conducted by the Whitetail Institute of North America, show an increase not only in the size of antlers, but also in body weight of deer in all categories and in fawn growth because of supplemental feeding programs and the development of high-quality food plots. The studies also show a decline in fawn mortality when a mineral-vitamin supplement program is instituted. Research has

This image captures what a field of dreams can do. Build it and they will come, stay, and grow bigger.

shown that supplemental feeding and high-quality food plots are effective across the whitetail's range.

One major benefit of proper nutrition is good skeletal growth. A deer's skeleton is not fully formed until three years of age. The body uses minerals such as phosphorus, calcium, and magnesium to grow and strengthen the skeletal system. Calcium and phosphorus are also critical for milk production in lactating does. These macrominerals, as well as trace minerals such as iron, zinc, copper, and selenium, are fundamentally important to good nutrition in white-tailed deer.

Antlers are extremely rapidly growing bones, extensions of the skeletal system. In the spring, hormonal changes in a buck cause antler buds to form. An accelerated antler growth phase takes place over the next several months, and vitamins and minerals are important in this process. Iron helps maintain the blood supply to the growing antlers. Copper aids collagen production, which supplies protein to the antlers. Phosphorus and calcium begin to be deposited in the antlers, giving them a solid structure. Toward the end of summer, more and more minerals are deposited as the mineralization process picks up speed. Eventually the blood supply is cut off from the antlers and the soft covering of velvet dries and peels away, revealing solid bone antlers that are approximately 55 percent mineral. This bone hat rack is what it's all about for the radical bowhunter—it's the stuff our dreams are made of.

Though this process creates those magnificent racks that we all pursue, it can have detrimental effects on the rest of the skeletal system. When a deer's body begins depositing large amounts of minerals in the growing antlers, much of the minerals are drawn from the internal skeletal system. Through its diet, the deer must replenish the calcium, phosphorus, and other minerals lost during the antler-building process. Producing antlers requires an incredible amount of minerals above and beyond the basic requirements for other body functions, and the larger the rack, the more minerals needed. Antler growth is always secondary to general body growth or health. A deer's antlers will be shortchanged if the animal is suffering from a deficiency of any nutrient.

Deer have varying needs for particular vitamins and nutrients for different physiological reasons, depending on the animal's sex and stage of the life cycle. Bucks need quality nutrition to support good antler growth, and lactating does need an abundance of minerals for milk production. Males have higher nutritional requirements for optimal body growth than females and are the first to show the ill effects of a poor diet. But they also respond more dramatically than females to improved nutrition. As nutrition improves, the difference in body size between male and female deer widens. Well-fed, mature bucks are 30 to 50 percent larger than does of similar age.

The rapid pace of a fawn's skeletal growth means that it, too, has exceptional requirements for minerals and vitamins. Protein is also important in a fawn's diet. Food-deprived fawns grow much more slowly and are structurally smaller, with smaller internal organs, but they have a surprising amount of fat. It appears that if general nutrition is poor, young deer will sacrifice body growth and shunt some nutrients into fat production instead of regular organ and skeletal growth.

Good nutrition is a lifetime requirement for growing trophy deer. Bucks grow their largest antlers when they are about five and a half years old, and most show a decline in antler size after nine and a half years. But if a whitetail buck is stunted at one and a half years of age, he will be undersize when full-grown and carry smaller-than-normal antlers.

Thus good mineral and vitamin levels are necessary not only for optimal antler growth, but also for a strong and healthy deer herd. An ample supply of essential nutrients is needed to produce quality deer, including those trophy bucks. If you give the deer a chance at optimal nutrition, you will reap big rewards come hunting season.

For one thing, white-tailed deer are larger in the North than the South. The southern or tropical subspecies have males that weigh only 40 to 50 pounds. Up north, some mature bucks tip the scales at 350 pounds or more. Large body size has been a selective trait among North American whitetails because it has special significance in relation to survival. During the long, harsh winters of the North, a large-bodied deer exposes less

A trio of bucks feeding in a narrow food plot created by the Whitetail Institute.

surface area in relation to its total body weight, thereby making it easier to stay warm. Retaining body heat more readily helps conserve a deer's energy. This can mean the difference between survival and death to a whitetail that experiences prolonged exposure to the harsh elements of a northern winter, especially if the only food source available is poor-quality browse. It's a fact that large-bodied deer go with large antlers, and you can expect to find larger bucks carrying larger antlers on northern ranges. Physiological factors such as nutrition, genetics, and age; social factors; and seasonal variations that affect food sources also play major roles in determining the size of both bucks and their antlers.

CREATING A HABITAT

Creating a habitat can be a daunting proposition unless you have legal access to an appropriate tract of land. If you are lucky and solvent enough to purchase a piece of good whitetail hunting property, you'll be off to a good start. If you're not able to purchase a piece of land, don't sell your home. Forcing the family to RV it while you grow a food plot is not going to endear you to your wife and kids. The radical bowhunter may be obsessed, but he's not that obsessed.

Actually, you may not need to buy the land. Some government programs offer different ways to use land for hunting purposes without actually purchasing it. For example, hunting access programs—in which the department of natural resources leases private property, especially agricultural land, for public hunting—are active in many states including Michigan. Another good option may be a lease. Just be sure to get a legal contract for a long-term lease with strong renewal clauses. After putting time, effort, and money into a piece of land, it would be a shame to lose the hunting rights or even the lease after your work is starting to pay off. Think about leasing with an option to buy, and consider creative financing with the landowner instead of working with a bank or other financial institution.

Another option for hunters and landowners is the Conservation Reserve Program (CRP), a voluntary program through which agricultural landowners receive annual rental payments and cost-share assistance in return for retiring land from farming and investing in long-term wildlife habitat development. To find out more about this program check the government website at www.fsa.usda.gov.

Once you have found a piece of land, make sure it is suitable for this purpose by doing an initial site survey. You may pay a consulting wildlife biologist to evaluate the property and give you an implementation plan, but you can check out the land on your own. Exploring the plot of land means walking the entire area. Carry a topographical map or GPS, and make notes as you go. Look for any existing and potential food sources. Try to determine what the deer are eating or browsing on and what they are *not* eating. Also look for a potential spot for a food plot. Are there any agricultural fields that can be easily plowed and tilled? Would a cutting and brush-clearing program open up the area to the regeneration of tender new growth? Would using a saw to fell or trim trees create a natural fence for the flow of deer through the area?

Once you've found a suitable property and studied it carefully, you can sit down and plan a strategy to create a big-buck factory. Your property needs to include several unique areas, because food alone is not enough to keep whitetails within your sights. It should have an area of thick cover to serve as secure sanctuary in addition to food plots and hunting areas.

Cover

An off-limits-to-humans, safe sanctuary area with lots of thick cover and a convenient food source will give deer in the area a place to hide, rest, and feed when humans have intruded for work detail or hunting. Post the area so that no one will enter. One quick way to provide instant cover is to drop unwanted trees at the end of summer. They will hold their leaves for months, affording lush cover. This cover provides more browse than bare ground. It can also make your property seem larger to a buck, because it can prevent his eyes from seeing habitat edges, and it will inhibit him from seeing you ascend a treestand or enter a ground blind.

Deer will use this area as a sanctuary when hunting pressure begins to be exerted. They will visit and revisit this area in times of pressure or stress, even years later when your big buck is ready for harvesting. The spot will become a familiar haven, and as long as it provides shelter, safety, and food, he will keep coming back to use it—and as he does, he will be presenting fantastic opportunities for you to harvest him as he arrives or leaves the haven.

Food Plot

Your big-buck factory also needs a food plot in order to provide the white-tails with good sources of nutrition throughout the year. Before you create a new food plot, work on enhancing the mast, browse, and food sources already in your hunting area. Fertilize native vegetation. Trim, prune, and fertilize fruit and nut trees to strengthen them and increase their harvests. If you own the land or plan on leasing long-term, consider planting some fruit or nut trees to provide some of the deer's favorite foods.

If the browse sources are old, dry, and depleted or it seems that the deer are not browsing in the area, aggressively cut and trim tree branches to open up the canopy. Closer to the ground, use a brush hog and chain saw to remove brush and cut down small trees. This will allow more sunlight to filter down to the understory and the ground, encouraging tender new growth.

Once you've beefed up what nature has provided, it's time to get to work on your food plot. Select the spot, based on the attributes you noted while exploring the plot of land. Ideally, the food plot should be placed in the center of your land for several reasons. More deer feeding there will stay there on your property, and while feeding, they will be obscured by the cover and trees around the plot. This helps hide your deer from other hunters as well as poachers. A centrally located plot also provides more security for the deer while they are foraging. If they feel secure, they will use your food plot more. Though this is the best-case scenario, if the food plot lies within one and a half to two miles of your hunting property, it will fulfill its purpose.

Cultivate, rototill, or manually turn up the soil. Have your soil tested at a local extension office or lab. The pH level should be between 6.5 and 7.0. If it is below 6.5, the soil it too acidic, and the vital nutrients needed for the plants to grow vigorously are lacking; add enough lime to bring your pH to the proper level. Lime is assimilated into the soil slowly, so

Food plots

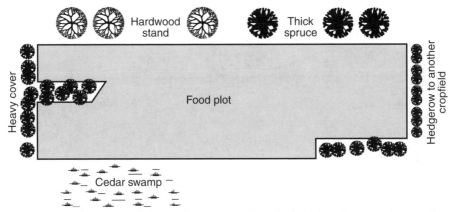

Food plots can be any size, from a few acres to hundreds, depending on how much land you have to manage and what you are trying to accomplish with your plan.

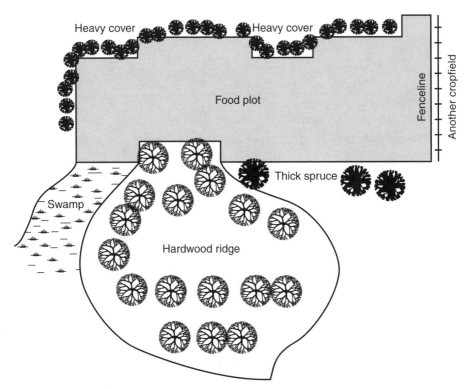

The key to a good food plot is to have as many inside and outside corners as possible so deer will feel comfortable as they enter and exit your plot.

Food plots

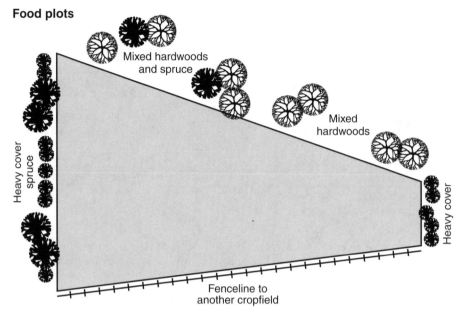

Any area that protrudes into the plot gives the deer time to survey the plot before venturing forth to feed in relative safety.

Hunting plots

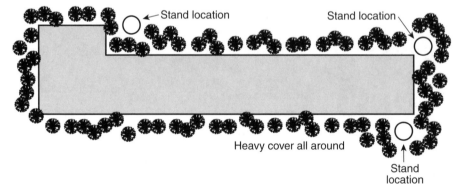

Hunting plots can be as small as half an acre long and very narrow. Thick cover surrounding the plot allows the radical bowhunter an opportunity to hunt inside or outside the corners. This arrangement also gives the whitetails more spots to enter and exit while feeling secure.

Hunting plots

A wagon-wheel hunting plot is a unique design that can be very productive. It works well with CRP fields grown in clear-cuts or brushy areas with dense woods or thick cover on one side. The spokes can be any length to fit the area you're planning to convert to a food plot.

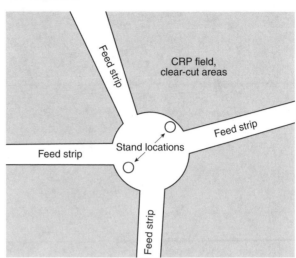

you lime this year for next year's growing season. If your soil is too acidic, it may take some time to bring the pH level up to where you need it. Most wooded areas need lime applications, so it is important to test the soil pH level throughout heavily forested tracts of land.

After tilling, prepare a smooth seed bed. Sow the seed with a broadcast spreader; even a hand-held one is fine. Hand-casting seed does not disperse the seed well. You want to provide an abundant supply of food that white-tailed deer prefer during every season. Products such as Whitetail Clover or Imperial Alfa-Rack will do the job nicely. Next, press the seed firmly into the ground with a roller or other tamping device. Wait for Mother Nature to provide the water, and seven to ten days after rain you should see signs of growth.

The need for a preferred source of food on or near your hunting land cannot be stressed enough. Studies at Georgia's Fort Perry Deer Research Facility show that most deer will reduce their home ranges to stay within half a mile of their most preferred food sources. If you plant these food sources and put in the time to manage them correctly, deer will change their travel patterns to come to the banquet you are providing.

Beef up the nutritional offerings of your feeding area by adding a mineral and vitamin supplement. A product such as Whitetail Institute's Imperial Whitetail 30-06 is an easy-to-use formula that will enhance your food plot by providing essential nutrients to your herd. You can also use mineral licks to supplement the deer's diet with additional vitamins and minerals.

It takes time and effort, but proper maintenance of a food plot will ensure that it stays in top condition.

Your plot requires regular maintenance in the form of mowing and fertilizing. When the plants reach a height of twelve to fifteen inches, clover should be mowed to a height of six to eight inches and Alfa-Rack around eight inches. Mowing serves two functions: It encourages tender new growth and minimizes weeds. You may want to use an herbicide to keep broad-leaved weeds down. Fertilize your plot in both early spring and autumn with about three hundred pounds of 0-20-20 fertilizer per acre.

Managing the Herd

Managing a white-tailed deer herd is much more complex and challenging than the average bowhunter may realize. That does not mean it is beyond your capabilities. Deer dispersal is one factor you need to consider when trying to manage a herd. Although it is true that subordinate bucks will be threatened by dominant bucks and sometimes leave their range, most bucks do not disperse because of other bucks. The main culprit in buck dispersal is frequently a doe. Usually dispersal begins when does force fawns away—generally when the young bucks are one and a half years old—just before or during the rut. When a young buck's mother kicks him out of the family group as she prepares to raise another

These two adjoining food plots are surrounded by timber and divided by a narrow strip of trees.

fawn, he is forced to find another home range. This forced dispersal can be lessened with an aggressive doe-harvesting program. The fewer does in the area, the fewer bucks will be forced away from your area, allowing them to stay, eat well, and grow.

By providing thick cover that offers an enticing and safe habitat, growing and enhancing food sources to make them the best possible, and aggressively harvesting does to minimize buck dispersal, you will make great strides toward holding bucks on your property, and you might be able to keep them around long enough that they will reap the benefits. As a blossoming radical bowhunter, you can be working on a hunting/food plot that will attract and keep deer in your area long enough to take advantage of the nutritious foodstuffs you are offering. You will also be able to grow your own trophy deer. As your herd remains hidden and safe on your land, the deer receive the gift of time that will help enable them to reach maturity and their full potential. You will also help create future generations of superior deer as each generation continues to improve under your care. At the same time, you will be honing your hunting skills and learning more about what it takes to become a radical bowhunter.

An early-November buck hitting a mock scrape set up less than fifty yards from a food plot.

RESOURCES

The following organizations can supply you with more specific information on creating your own big-buck factory.

The Whitetail Institute of North America
239 Whitetail Trail
Pintala, AL 36043
800-688-3030
www.whitetailinstitute.com

Quality Deer Management Association (QDMA)
P.O. 160
Bogart, GA 30622
800-209-3337
www.qdma.com

North Country Whitetails
700 N. Main Street
Newark, NY 14513
315-331-6959
www.northcountrywhitetails.com

CHAPTER 3

Finding a Big Buck

If you can't go to the big-buck promised land and you don't have the property to manage, you can still bag a big buck. This chapter will help you find him where you hunt. Finding trophy bucks has taken me everywhere on the map in recent years, including many urbanized areas like Greenwich, Connecticut, where, although the acreage of habitat is very limited, at least a few bucks grow trophy-class headgear every year. I've also hunted for big bucks in spots that are more remote, far away from the big cities, like Sweet Grass, Saskatchewan, which has pumped out trophy after trophy. The radical bowhunter takes advantage of the possibility of finding these monsters, all across North America, leaving no stone unturned, no thicket unscouted, and no spot summarily dismissed.

Don't you just love all the magazine articles explaining "Ten Tips to Get Your Buck Every Year" or "The Yellow Brick Road to Trophy Bucks"? They want us to believe by reading this stuff, harvesting a trophy buck is as simple as walking into the woods and climbing into a treestand. But in the real world, there are no magic bullets, no easy solutions, and no sure-fire shortcuts to harvesting trophy whitetails with a bow. Getting that big buck requires lots of hard work, many hours of the proper preparation, unlimited patience, total persistence, and full dedication to the sport of bowhunting. Given the small number of trophy-class white-tailed deer seen by most hunters during their entire hunting careers, you might even think that harvesting an officially scored record-book buck is a lot like winning the lottery or hitting it big in Las Vegas. But bagging a trophy is more than just luck—you must work to put the odds in your favor, and you have to be selective about the deer you harvest. The radical bowhunter carefully considers the deer potential of a hunting area, invests a great deal of time in scouting the area, and commits considerable time to hunting in order to have a decent opportunity to be in the right place at the right time to harvest that trophy buck.

To be able to harvest a big buck, you must hunt where these trophy deer exist. So it follows that the more big bucks are living in the area you hunt, the better your chances are to bag one. Age, genetics, and habitat are the three key ingredients in producing trophy white-tailed deer—nothing has ever changed that holy trinity. Other factors also affect the ability of the land you hunt to produce trophy-class whitetail bucks, such as hunting pressure, a well-balanced buck-to-doe ratio, and maybe a little bit of luck.

Once you get a crack at a real trophy buck, the experience will change your attitude forever. When you decide to get serious about putting a tag on a monster buck, you will quickly come to realize that a lot of effort is required before and after the bow season. Activities such as doing research and familiarizing yourself with and testing new equipment before you even set foot in the field all take time and effort. The radical bowhunter will not shirk these less-than-glamorous responsibilities in becoming totally prepared for the hunt of a lifetime. The knowledge you have obtained will be the driving force behind successfully bagging that trophy buck of your dreams.

With so many choices, how does one know what to do or where to start? You have to have a goal with a specific plan; otherwise you will be running around like a dog chasing his tail. You'll be wasting time wondering where to go or just wandering around on a piece of property that probably never had the potential to produce the trophy buck you want.

FINDING AN AREA WITH BIG BUCKS

Even though there are no easy ways or shortcuts to put that big buck on the ground, hunting specific locations where monster bucks live will greatly increase your odds. There are four different information sources that you should use to help you pick the best place to concentrate your hunting effort. Each one provides a different piece of the puzzle. Doing a side-by-side comparison of the data from all of these sources should reveal patterns or trends that point to which area or specific county in your state or province has been producing the best and most bucks with trophy racks. This data can really help you zero in on a big-buck honey hole if used properly.

Start your information gathering by joining the Boone and Crockett and Pope and Young Clubs' Associate Membership programs. You will start getting these organizations' quarterly newsletters, which list all the current entries into the record books during that quarter. This is the most up-to-date information on where trophy bucks have been harvested. You

The third Bay State buck I harvested from the same honey hole.
JOHN DZIZA

need this type of timely data, not old or historical information. The data in these organizations' record books is likely outdated, because both clubs publish new record books on a six-year cycle.

Things change quickly in hunting areas, and I have not yet seen a change for the better. New hot spots get publicity, and hunters flock in and clear out the area or apply so much pressure that the whitetails hightail it to a safer location. You want to hunt an area while it is hot, then move on to the next. This is one reason why I'm always on the search for new areas to hunt big bucks.

The second source of information you should explore is the state or provincial record books for a given area. They can be very helpful in your search for that big-buck promised land. The ease of obtaining information varies from state to state. In some cases, you can simply go online and get all the data you need; other times, you might have to make some calls or drive to a library or state office building where the record books or other data are stored. Because these are public, taxpayer-supported organizations, they are required to share the information they gather, though in some cases you might have to pay a fee for photocopying or other services.

Winter is a great time to fly over an area to investigate the deer population and do some off-season scouting. This photo was taken in Massachusetts while making a deer count of a new area. The backdrop of snow makes deer highly visible.

The third place to search out information is sportsmen's shows or deer classics. Many state organizations have booths at these events, allowing you to approach wildlife officials in a friendly setting and ask about getting the data you want. Typically, official measurers are on hand to measure trophy bucks, and you will be able to ask them where the good bucks have been coming from in your area. It's called networking, and it really works. Most of these people will be glad to share this information with you, and you may even end up with a good future contact or friend.

The final source of information to consider is your area's deer biologist. These professionals know where the most big bucks are coming from each year, even down to fairly exact locations. Many of them also produce annual reports with harvest figures by county and town, which are available to you free or for a minimal fee.

None of this information will tell you which tree to hang your treestand on or where to place your ground blind, but it is a giant step in the right direction. You will have to dig a little deeper once you have narrowed your search down to one or two specific locations.

In addition to hard work, attitude is an important ingredient in your overall success. A person who thinks of money all the time is the one that gets wealthy. The fisherman that always catches big fish is the guy who has catching big fish on his mind all the time, always uses the right lure or fly, and is in the best part of the water fishing. Radical bowhunters think about big deer all the time. To be consistently successful, killing big bucks has to be a big part of you life or you will fail. Set your standards high and don't be satisfied with anything less from then on in your bowhunting career. This mindset will help you come a long way in becoming a radical bowhunter. The proper attitude will take you many places during the course of your life and bowhunting big bucks is just one of them.

PRIVATE LAND

Once you locate an area that has trophy buck potential, go out of your way to find some good private land on which to bowhunt. This may take some effort, but it will be well worth it in the long run. Spend some time learning who the landowners are in your target area. Make a personal visit well in advance of the hunting season opener and ask permission. It's best to meet face-to-face rather than send a letter. When you go, dress in nice casual clothes, not camouflage, in order to present a good image. Many landowners feel that bowhunters are more responsible than gun hunters. But remember, it's all in the presentation. Let them know that you are a very responsible bowhunter and offer to give references. Be polite. You might even ask if you can help with any chores around the place, such as trimming or fence mending. Let them know that you will watch over the property as if it were your own, and if you witness anything out of place, you will bring it to their attention immediately. I once obtained permission from a farmer by helping him post his land so nobody could hunt the property but me.

Don't forget the landowners after the season is over. Give them a little something for Christmas: a bottle of wine, a gift certificate for a restaurant. Don't forget the lady of the house; an elegant box of chocolates or a plant will show your appreciation to her as well. These little acts of gratitude will go a long way toward building a relationship so that you can gain long-term access to the property. Take it from this radical bowhunter—a little extra effort will reap big benefits.

PUBLIC LAND

If no private land is available, harvesting a trophy-class buck on public land is a realistic possibility if you go about it properly. Success on public land takes planning, setting a goal, studying resources, and devoting plenty of time to hunting in the woods. Opening day of gun season at some public hunting areas in my home state resembles the parking lot at

This trophy buck was harvested from a satellite area in my home state of Massachusetts. The area has great potential, and gaining access to one of these less pressured areas can make the difference to a radical bowhunter. JOHN DZIZA

Yankee Stadium during the playoffs. In the woods, all the hunter orange makes it look like sunrise in a pumpkin patch. Needless to say, such areas rarely produce big bucks because of the pressure they receive every year. Here again, advance research will pay off for you. Most hunters head to the well-known state forests or wildlife management areas, but few people realize that popular spots often have satellite areas, nearby tracts of land, sometimes with poor access, that are open to public hunting but are not publicized. They can be real honey holes, with few people hunting the area.

In my home state of Massachusetts, several state forests have tremendous satellite areas. Many of these are properties of about three to four hundred acres that were bought by the state back in the late 1940s for nonpayment of taxes. I have taken several 140-class or better bucks from these properties over the years. Several of them are in towns with private property that is otherwise closed to hunting except for written permission—and getting written permission would almost take an act of God.

Getting permission to hunt private property has become more difficult. Today's landowners don't always see the white-tailed deer as a pest, but rather as an asset to their property. Nonetheless, getting permission to hunt private property is not impossible and is often worth the effort. Here are some tips to help you succeed:

- First impressions are important. Always be very clean and neatly dressed when going to ask permission.
- Ask permission well in advance of the time you want to hunt the property.
- Plan your visit right after lunch or early in the evening when the landowner, especially a farmer, will most likely be at home.
- Ask permission by yourself or with one other person—never take a gang up to the landowner's door.
- Always offer the landowner some venison once you have an animal butchered.

If you are unable to find one of these places to hang your stand or erect your ground blind, use topographic and aerial maps and get back into the deep woods to get away from the crowd. Most hunters won't take the time to get way back into the woods because they do not want to haul all their gear that far. They may also have fears of getting lost in the woods. They could be reluctant to drag or pack out a deer the long distance through rough country. Because they don't think the effort is worth the reward, they miss the opportunity to hunt bucks that have been pushed back into the deep woods to avoid pressure. These deer are totally unpressured, and that alone will be a big factor in your favor. Be radical. Use a mountain bike or a canoe on a river or lake if necessary, but get back there and capitalize on the average hunter's laziness.

Once you have picked the spot or spots you plan to bowhunt, purchase a few quality scouting cameras. Place them in strategic locations before the season and keep them up even into the season. (Turn to chapter 9 for a detailed explanation of using scouting cameras, an important tool in the radical bowhunter's arsenal.) By watching the deer in each area I have covered with a scouting camera, I can determine several key pieces

Scouting cameras placed in strategic locations before and during hunting season can save hours of time and effort when scouting a new area. They are not intrusive and will not disturb the whitetails in the area.

WILDLIFE RESEARCH CENTER

of information, such as how many bucks are in that area, what spot has the biggest buck on the property, and the area's buck-to-doe ratio. This will save you hours of legwork, and you will not risk blowing the deer out of the area and repatterning the big buck you want to hunt.

Finding and killing a trophy buck has never been an easy task. You can turn to a host of methods, including voodoo or fortune tellers, or you can make a concerted research effort and rely more on reliable information about where to find trophy bucks and less on Lady Luck.

PART TWO

WHEN:

Stack the odds in your favor by hunting big bucks when they are most vulnerable

CHAPTER 4

Early-Season Ambush

Big bucks are relatively vulnerable while still in their late-summer bachelor groups, especially if you've identified preferred routes to their favorite food source. As the hunting season approaches, two profound facts remain true: Before a hunter can harvest any deer, he or she must first create the opportunity to shoot it; and before a hunter can shoot a deer, it must be within range of the hunter's bow. This may be stating the obvious, but few hunters really understand these statements.

Year after year, hunters descend on the woods, ascend their treestands, in the same places they've put them for years, and come home empty-handed. They are forgetting that if they want to kill big bucks, they have to be adaptable to every situation. Furthermore, the key to success is knowing exactly where to place that treestand—but do all great hunting spots have a tree? Although stand hunting remains the most popular whitetail bowhunting technique, there are times and places where it is impossible to set up a treestand. In those situations, the bowhunter must adapt to the situation and use another method to get that buck.

Several years ago, I was hunting a really nice buck in southern Iowa and had seen the buck twice from my treestand. Both times he was way out of range for a shot. He was coming up through a bottom along a strip of new-growth trees and crossing into a large cornfield. There was no place to move my stand that would put me in a better position, because where I needed to be offered no trees large enough to accommodate a stand. I looked the situation over for a long time. Finally it dawned on me that I had to move to the cover of the cornfield and put up a ground blind. Many hunters would not even consider hunting from anything other than a treestand, but not so with the radical bowhunter. After putting up the blind, I waited only two mornings before this big buck showed himself again. I was able to put an arrow through him

This corn-fed buck was taken at eighteen yards from a ground blind that concealed me in the corner of a cornfield. JOHN DZIZA

at eighteen yards just as he headed into the cornfield. It was the perfect ambush situation.

It is true that many hunters just pick a spot and allow luck to guide their hunt. Many are successful, but for consistent results, especially on mature whitetail bucks, a radical bowhunter needs to rely on knowledge and experience to help him locate the best possible ambush point—or several points, for that matter. Using your knowledge of a white-tailed deer's basic bodily functions will help you locate a possible area and enable you to predict the pattern of behavior of the buck in the area during the early season before all the leaves have fallen. Then your experience in the woods will enable you to pull all the information together so that you can select a good site for your treestand or blind.

After velvet shedding is complete, it is unlikely for mature bucks to venture forth into open fields during the daylight hours. Use a spotting scope to glass fields in August.

A buck has three main functions that determine his activities and travel patterns: eating, sleeping, and mating. Understanding how these functions work is critical in the formation of any ambush strategy, but in the early season, eating is the most important function.

Learning as much as you can about the area or habitat is key, and one thing you need to learn is where the preferred foods of the deer can be found. Deer need foods that are high in protein and carbohydrates to meet their nutritional requirements. Learning what types of food offer these nutrients and their seasonal availability is extremely important. A white-tailed deer's natural instincts let him know what types of foods are best for him, and he will in effect eat what he needs.

Just after the bucks shed their velvet, especially the mature dominant bucks, they seem to disappear or go into hiding. You do not see them out in fields during daylight hours. Does, being biologically different, continue along with their normal movements. Because of this behavioral change, early-season bowhunting can become frustrating. But this can be a great time to be out there, because the bucks are in their bachelor groups, and multiple bucks often travel together. Once the rut arrives, these bachelor groups will be broken up, and the bucks will have no set patterns in their movements. They will be continually on the move looking for or following a hot doe.

FOOD SOURCES

Bucks increase their body weight by almost 25 percent during September and early October. They seem to have an inborn mechanism that prepares them for the rigors of the November rutting period and all activity it brings. So the key to locating bucks during this period is to scout the area for the main food sources. The white-tailed deer's food preferences vary across the country and may include acorns (especially from the white oak), beechnuts, persimmons, mushrooms, Japanese honeysuckle, corn, clover, kudzu, fall-planted grainfields, and abandoned orchards, especially apple. Each one of these could present a hot spot to ambush a good buck during the early season.

Old, abandoned apple trees are a good bet, especially if they are isolated, because they present a food pocket that will concentrate the bucks in one place. The ideal ambush setup requires adequate cover around the food source and multiple escape routes for the deer. If it does not offer these features, bucks will only visit the area at night and not during legal hunting hours. If a single tree has lots of apples on it, is surrounded by cover, and has ample deer sign around it, it might be a good place to set up a treestand or even a ground blind. If the area has several trees with a lot of apples, you need to identify a setup location that bucks must pass to get to the apple trees. Another great setup location is near a white oak that is producing a bumper crop of acorns. To determine exactly where deer will be positioned when feeding, look for ground littered with acorns and look up into the tree, using binoculars if needed, to spot acorns that have not fallen. Also look for large amounts of deer droppings on the ground.

Fields of alfalfa, clover, rye, and even wheat can be very productive ambush locations. The problem with these fields is that the bucks usually come out into them only after shooting light. But if the field is small and has ample cover around it, bucks will enter them during the last few hours of shooting light and in the very early morning. The setup for these fields should be at least fifty yards back into the cover from the field edge, at a location where several good, heavily used trails intersect each other. These locations seem to be much better for afternoon than morning hunts. Bucks often move into these areas during last light, feed throughout the night without moving too far, and then head back to bedding areas before or just at dawn.

One fall in Mississippi, I was hunting over a small, isolated clover field way back in the woods. Making it even better, there had been several inches of rain the week before, and much of the area was flooded. This area was almost inaccessible by vehicle, but we found a way to get into it

During the early season, bucks are still in bachelor groups, and more than one buck may walk by your stand if you take the necessary precautions to conceal yourself.

on my last night. I saw seventeen different bucks that night, from spike horns to a couple nice ten-pointers, before the end of shooting light. As luck would have it, the bigger bucks never came within range during shooting light, and I had to leave the following morning. This was a great ambush spot where someone could put a tag on a nice buck, though unfortunately that time it was not meant to be me.

Many bowhunters make a big mistake by overhunting one early-season ambush location. If you overhunt one spot, you risk repatterning the bucks or pushing them out of the area completely. A radical bowhunter finds several prime food locations that the bucks are using so he does not overhunt one place and ruin the spot. Armed with all of this information, look for the food sources in your hunting area and begin to form your ambush strategy.

BEDDING
The next logical step is to try to determine possible bedding sites within the buck's core area. In the early season, bedding areas are secondary to food sources when selecting ambush sites. Nonetheless, it can be to your advantage to identify the places where deer bed down after feeding. Deer will seek out bedding areas where they can use the wind and air currents to their advantage. Learn about the geographic contours of the land to aid

Bag your buck during the early season. This big guy was taken on the first day of the season from a perfect ambush site. JOHN DZIZA

you in locating potential sites. In the morning, deer will be high on ridges or hills. The rising sun warms the air, and as it warms, it rises, bringing with it a world of sensory information to the deer's keen nose. The reverse is true in the evening, when deer descend to lower elevations. During a warm and humid spell, the weather both enhances a deer's sense of smell and increases the production of human scents. Scent control is an absolute must during the early season, when bucks can wind a human from much farther distances than later in the season.

Remember one important factor before shifting your ambush focus from food sources to bedding areas: Changes in the weather increase a deer's activity. Whitetails can sense when the weather is going to shift, and if they feel a storm coming, they will feed long and hard to make up for the time they must remain in the safety and security of their bedding areas as they wait out bad weather.

WAITING

Once you find your ambush spots, you face the challenge that many hunters find the most difficult: the watchful waiting. Many hunters pop in and out of their treestands at various times for different reasons. Some hunt only in the early morning and late afternoon to evening. Others get restless and head out for lunch. Spending as much time as possible in your stand will increase your chances of sighting deer, especially as a buck wanders to meet does or changes his feeding pattern to meet changing weather conditions. If you spend every minute you can in your ambush spot, you will not only increase your chances of bagging a buck, but you'll also be increasing your knowledge, which will pay off in seasons to come. Sitting in a treestand can be tough, but early-season mild weather should help make it a pleasant experience. The leaves are changing color and the spectacular smells of autumn fill the deer woods—not a bad place to pass the time.

CHAPTER 5

Using the Moon to Predict the Rut

Humans have long credited the moon with controlling or contributing to happenings on earth. Some of these theories have been proven. We know that the gravitational pull of the moon directly affects the tides. Native Americans used moon phases to schedule planting and harvesting, and this accurate natural calendar is still published each year in the *Farmers' Almanac*. Moon phases also seem to influence white-tailed deer behavior. Research has shown that the lunar cycle is the basis for the estrous cycle of the whitetail doe, and some believe that the waxing and waning of the silvery orb can have an impact on deer feeding and movement patterns as well.

Hunters' records indicate that there may be truth to this theory. Plus, it seems logical that as nocturnal creatures, sensitive to low-light conditions, white-tailed deer would be attuned to the moon and its phases. Formal research does suggest a link between lunar cycles and whitetail behavior, though the moon does not play as important of a role as other determinants, such as weather, doe-to-buck ratio, and the deer's general health. Nonetheless, examining whitetail behavior relative to the moon is another technique that a radical bowhunter can use to help formulate an overall hunting strategy. Tying rut behavior to moon phases appears to have particular promise. Before putting the technique to work, it is important to first monitor a buck's activity patterns in the days leading up to the start of mating season.

PRERUT ACTIVITY

Before the rut begins, feeding is a whitetail buck's primary autumn activity in preparation for the physical demands of the breeding cycle as well as the severity of winter. Bucks feed heavily and put on extra weight. In addition to bulking up, the white-tailed deer is undergoing behavioral and physical changes in response to the changing amounts of daylight. Photoperiodicity drives nature's timetable, from leaves dropping to antler growth.

In mid-September, antler velvet dries, cracks, and peels. The buck's testosterone levels are just high enough to inspire rubbing. As the levels increase at the end of September, scraping begins. In mid-October, testosterone levels are still increasing and bucks are moving during the daylight hours. At this time, the does' estrogen levels climb and they begin to smell different. By early November, both sexes have peaked and the stage is set for the rut—that crazy and frenzied two-week period in a whitetail's life where everything that preceded actual breeding was related. We all know how crazy a guy can get over a female, and the whitetail buck is no different.

Velvet peeling, rubbing, scraping, and fighting all help strengthen a dominant buck and prepare him for breeding. Because of the heavy feeding activity, bucks are fat-laden. They'll need this fat, as a dominant breeder buck can lose as much as 25 percent of his body weight as he focuses on breeding instead of on feeding or survival. It is at this time when he is most vulnerable.

Before he is ready to seek, breed, and tend, a buck must assert his dominance on his turf. As his antlers harden, his rubbing becomes more frequent, and he strengthens his neck and shoulder muscles. He is also leaving visual and scent markers, and other bucks know he's been in the vicinity. He makes scrapes to leave as a calling card, allowing him to deposit his scent throughout its area.

PUTTING THE MOON TO WORK

To use the moon phases to predict deer behavior, you need to accurately log the timing of deer movement and sightings along with lunar phase information. Keeping these records will let you determine how helpful this technique is. If you enjoy learning as much as possible from other hunters and statistical information, you can also analyze record books for their time-of-day harvest information and compare this with the moon phases to try to establish a trend for your area.

Hunters should be concerned primarily with two moon phases, the full and the new moon, which seem to have opposite effects on whitetail behavior. The full moon has long been thought to be a bad time to hunt deer, because the increased moonshine would allow for more nocturnal feeding. But research appears to suggest that the converse is true. Though the whitetails are able to see better in these more illuminating conditions, their predators enjoy the same advantage, so the deer instinctively become more cautious. They sneak about in the shadows, trying to remain undetected, and then feed the following day. During full-moon phases, deer movement usually increases around midday, from approximately 10 A.M. to 3 P.M. There is also some secondary movement early in the morning and late in the evening. The dark of the new moon provides more protection, and during this phase the movement pattern is generally reversed, with the most significant activity in the early morning and late evening and considerably less movement in the middle of the day.

If you have only a limited amount of time to spend hunting, you can use this knowledge to appropriately adjust the times you hunt. If your hunting day happens to fall when the moon has waned and a new moon is in the sky, early morning and late afternoon should be the most productive. If it's a full moon, hunt during midday to increase your chances of spotting and harvesting a deer.

This moonshine scheme is straightforward and easy to incorporate into your present style of hunting.

There are no quick answers in the quest for a trophy whitetail, just an ongoing commitment to learn as much as possible about the behavior of the deer and the area where you plan to hunt. That coupled with practice blend together to take the hunter into the whitetail's world as a smarter, more prepared adversary.

Beyond this relatively simple full-moon, new-moon premise is another theory of how the lunar cycles affect whitetail behavior.

Wayne Laroche, wildlife biologist and current commissioner of the Vermont Fish and Wildlife Department, has developed some other fascinating theories regarding the moon phases and the whitetail rut. Although latitude is largely responsible for determining the rut season in the higher latitudes, Laroche hypothesizes that photoperiodicity, or the amount of daylight, is the trigger and moonlight is the environmental cue that synchronizes the estrous cycle and triggers the rut.

Laroche has developed a whitetail rut prediction table that gives hunters the most accurate time for the peak of the rut, more specific than the general November 15 date that we use in the North. The table incorporates the effects of the lunar phases on the doe's estrous cycle and maps out the corresponding rut behavior exhibited by bucks. A radical bowhunter can use this information to help plan hunting strategies throughout the fall. The rut makes a whitetail buck more vulnerable, and knowing exactly when it will kick in allows a radical bowhunter to take advantage of the best window of opportunity. Three phases of behavior are evident in the whitetail male during the rut: seeking, chasing, and tending and breeding. As the rut proceeds through these phases of predictable behaviors, you can anticipate the type of behavior and adjust your hunting strategy to be most effective.

Seeking

Seeking behavior begins at the onset of the rut, when bucks begin to look for does. In the North, this occurs at about the time of the November full moon. A buck is more vocal now than at any other time of the year, communicating with grunts, bleats, snorts, and wheezes.

Whitetail bucks spend much time and travel many miles in search of does. They walk slowly into the wind, as smell is the primary sense they use to find does. You may see aggressive behavior between bucks as they enlarge their territories in search of hot does. This high-level seeking and searching makes hunting from a treestand an effective technique at this time. Increased movement means greater odds of a buck meandering by your stand. Bucks during this time may be enticed with calls, rattling, decoys, and scents.

Of all the times to hunt, the seeking phase is best, especially for a treestand hunter. A radical bowhunter in the northern U.S. will hunt the optimal time from three to four days before until two to three days after the November full moon. Bucks are on the move but do not yet chase every doe they see. They will pass through funnels, walk along edges, and visit and revisit their rub and scrape lines. Their movement patterns are more predictable in this phase, so a radical bowhunter will take advantage of that before the real craziness begins.

Chasing

Many deer hunters get confused between the seeking behavior phase and the chasing behavior phase of the rutting cycle because they overlap each other. Chasing behavior starts approximately two days after the rutting moon, as soon as a buck finds a doe that is approaching estrus, and continues for up to four full days, running right into the breeding phase of the rutting cycle.

At first, the doe will run off as the buck nears. She does not flee for her life but plays coy, dashing ahead and then slowing down, stopping, and looking back for the pursuing buck. This continues until the doe is receptive enough to let the buck remain with her. Your stand should be located in a doe's home territory at this time. It's a great place to be, as more than one buck may take up the chase.

Though the chasing phase can be a great time to hunt, it can also be frustrating. As the bucks chase those does, they can cover huge amounts of territory. This may move a trophy you've targeted far out of his home range.

This buck is on the trail of a doe that is not quite receptive enough to breed. He will follow her relentlessly until the time is right.

Tending and Breeding

Once a doe allows a buck to remain with her, tending behavior begins. While tending, a buck will stick close to a doe until she is bred. Usually this behavior lasts about seventy-two hours, and then the buck immediately reverts to more seeking behavior. Tending behavior peaks about the time of the new moon during rut periods. When breeding actively begins, about five to seven days after the November full moon in the North, it will last about fourteen days, during which 70 to 80 percent of mature does will be bred. Scrape activity nearly ceases, and seeking and chasing are limited. The dominant breeder bucks never rest or eat, devoting their time to breeding and trying to run off intruders. Bucks can seem to virtually disappear as they stay close to the does, moving only when the does move. As females cover little ground, deer activity can seem to come to a screeching halt. During this time, if you find a doe, you'll find a buck.

This is the most difficult time to hunt because of the limited movement. A radical bowhunter will set up a treestand in the hot doe's core area or in sites that are known to be frequented by doe groups. This may be one time when it's okay to get out of your treestand, as tracking can be effective for pursuing a tending buck that is focused on a doe. Bucks also tend to respond to grunt calls as they rush to drive off interlopers.

This dominant buck is guarding his hot doe. He is on alert to drive off all intruders. JOHN DZIZA

PREDICTING THE RUT

Laroche believes that moonlight transmits signals to the doe's endocrine system, causing increased or decreased production of the hormones that affect the estrous cycle. The phases of the moon occur on a recurring cycle that is similar to the twenty-eight-day estrous cycle of a whitetail doe.

In the North, when the November full moon fills the sky, a buck's breeding instincts are in full swing. The doe's reproductive cycle kicks in about a week later. Therefore, the period of the waxing moon, the full moon, and the waning moon may indicate optimum rutting activity, though the peak of the rut can also be affected by weather or hunting pressure.

I harvested this monster at the peak of the rut during a new moon. JOHN DZIZA

Even though a doe's estrous cycle begins about a week after the November full moon, most does enter estrus as the third quarter phase of the moon wanes and the total dark of the new moon nears. When scrape activity by bucks falls off, that's a signal to hunters that the breeding phase has begun.

A secondary rut follows about twenty-eight days behind the first one, as it is triggered by those does that did not conceive or were not bred during the primary rut. It follows the same basic cycle, just a full moon later. Hunting during the secondary rut can be extremely difficult. The hormones that had bucks flying a few weeks earlier are slowing down, and they are calmer. They may be physically exhausted and looking to recoup some of their lost weight. Many bucks limit their movements to nighttime or the fringes of daylight as they seek to restore themselves. A radical bowhunter will intensely hunt food sources that are close to thick cover, as well as buck bedding areas and associated escape routes.

In recent years, hunters have become increasingly aware of whitetail behavior. We have become more scientific in our approach to whitetail hunting as new innovations and modern technology meet to provide us with not only more information than ever before but new techniques and devices to aid us in the pursuit of whitetails. These moon theories are simply a new way to explain behaviors that hunters have observed for a long time, but maybe hadn't even thought to connect to an external force. We now know that the moon affects many things on our planet, and research is beginning to show that white-tailed deer estrous cycles and rutting behavior are among them.

Laroche used to provide a product called the Whitetail Rut Predictor, but *Deer and Deer Hunting* magazine now publishes the material in its annual white-tailed deer calendar. Two books have been written using the research that Laroche has collected over the many years of his studies on how the moon affects the whitetail rut.

SUMMARY

- The movement of white-tailed deer can be predicted from year to year, using the phases of the moon. This is most valuable to bowhunters with limited amounts of time to hunt.
- The best time to be in the woods if you want to kill a buck is from a few days before to a few days after the new moon.
- The worst time to hunt white-tailed deer is from just before to just after the first quarter of the moon.

RESOURCES

White-Tailed Deer Calendar
Deer and Deer Hunting
800-258-0929
www.krause.com

Hunting Whitetails by the Moon
by Charles Alsheimer, Krause Publications, 1999
800-258-0929
www.krause.com

Moon Struck
by Jeff Murray, Fool Moon Press, 1996
800-449-6645
www.moonguide.com

CHAPTER 6

Hunting by the Weather

A radical bowhunter knows that on any given day, weather is the single most important factor affecting white-tailed deer activity. Understanding how the weather can trigger this activity ensures that you'll be in the deer woods on those magic days.

The best way to pattern a good buck using the weather is to begin keeping accurate records of weather conditions every time you enter the deer woods to hunt or even scout. If you start making this a part of every trek, it will enable you to zero in more closely on that trophy buck you're after. Carry a simple notepad for taking notes in the field. At home, you can enter your notes into a good computer hunting log book, such as the DeerTrack Hunting Log, which will cross-reference the data automatically as you add information over time. These records will take the guesswork out of connecting deer behavior to weather conditions and refute the old wives' tales.

Biologists have confirmed that weather conditions affect the daily movement of the white-tailed deer, but many disagree about which is the most important factor that triggers their activity. Nothing can dispute your own documented observations of the weather conditions in your deer woods. Keeping accurate records lets you draw your own conclusions, based on your own experiences in your own hunting area.

Which weather condition has the most impact on white-tailed deer movement, or do they all play an equal part? Does rain enhance your opportunities or decrease your odds of seeing a buck and getting a shot? Will you see more deer activity when the barometer is falling or rising? Is wind or temperature more important? How do atmospheric conditions such as cloud cover, fog, or storm fronts influence deer behavior? All of those variations in the weather can affect your hunt.

Analyzing the weather conditions is a more than just a good tool for choosing which days to hunt. Many bowhunters do not have the luxury of picking their hunting days. When they hit the field is dependent on work schedules, vacation time, or fixed travel arrangements for a hunt in a distant state, and they find themselves at the mercy of the weather. It is important to understand how a white-tailed deer reacts to different weather conditions so you can adapt your hunting plans accordingly.

BAROMETRIC PRESSURE

Purchasing a barometer is a very worthwhile investment. Most successful bowhunters pay close attention to the barometric pressure as an indication of white-tailed deer activity. This is the number-one factor to watch when you are heading off to bowhunt. Reading the barometer each day before you hunt will give you a good idea of the amount of whitetail activity you can expect to see.

Simply stated, when the barometer is on the rise, indicating high pressure moving into the area after a storm, or shows a steady high reading, you can generally expect the best deer activity. When the barometer is falling or shows steady low pressure, indicating a storm or changing weather approaching, the deer usually are hanging tight and not moving about.

TEMPERATURE

The relationship between temperature and deer activity is clearly understood. Deer movement usually decreases when the thermometer reads higher than 50 to 55 degrees F in the North and 60 to 70 degrees in the South. As a general rule, the warmer it gets, the less daylight movement. In warm weather, deer move mostly during the low-light periods of the day and after dark, when the temperatures are much cooler.

Conversely, low temperatures stimulate daytime activity. Generally, when the temperature is lower than minus 10 degrees in the far north and 25 degrees in the South, deer activity increases during the warmest hours of the day. I saw this happen on a Saskatchewan hunt when the temperature dipped below minus 30 degrees for three straight days and deer activity dramatically increased between 10 A.M. and 2 P.M. It was warmer during that part of the day, and the deer did not have to use as much energy to move around.

WIND

Paying attention to the wind in your hunting area will help you understand how deer react to variations in the wind conditions. When the air

These deer are feeding early in the day as a high-pressure system moves in following a heavy rain. Weather is the most important factor affecting whitetail activity.

ranges from dead calm up to about fifteen miles per hour, deer generally move about freely. At these lower wind speeds, the type of wind is much more important than the wind velocity relative to deer movement. Most whitetails will tolerate a steady breeze even if it is strong, but they dislike gusty winds that change direction frequently. Such winds seem to affect their senses of hearing and smell, two of their most critical survival tools, and they get very nervous about their surroundings.

Once the velocity exceeds about fifteen miles per hour, deer start to slow down their movements. As wind speed approaches twenty to twenty-five miles per hour, deer activity tends to decrease dramatically. The exception to this rule can be found in areas where wind velocity is regularly higher than normal. In windy regions, deer will have adapted to the environmental conditions, because realistically they have to in order to survive.

FOG AND LIGHT RAIN

When I was a kid hunting ducks with my dad, I quickly realized that the worse skies looked in the morning, the more ducks we saw. The same is true with the white-tailed deer. Atmospheric conditions such as fog, mist, rain, and snow—or the lack of them—all have an effect on how the deer will move. Fog and rain tend to deaden light, noise, and all the things that

I took this 8-pointer in heavy cover adjacent to a feed area as a frontal system approached.

stimulate a deer's wary senses. The low light, in particular, seems to encourage deer to bed down later in the morning and move earlier during the afternoon. A day with heavy ground fog or even a light, misty rain usually provides the best conditions a bowhunter could ask for in the deer woods.

STORMS

Hunters can take advantage of quick-passing frontal systems, which often produce some spectacular weather events involving plenty of high wind and rain. These conditions create some fantastic bowhunting opportunities, but the key is timing. When you know a storm is approaching, plan to hunt all around it—before, during, and after. A white-tailed deer knows before we do that the weather is going to change soon, even without the Weather Channel, but they don't know how long the storm will last.

As soon as deer feel the barometric pressure start to drop, regardless of the time of day, they will start to feed heavily. Because the deer let their guard down a little, the odds can favor the hunter in these situations. A radical bowhunter targets feeding areas close to heavy cover or the major trails leading to them, setting up just ahead of the approaching frontal system. During the early season, whitetails feed on various crops in agricultural fields as well as mast crops such as acorns and beechnuts. As the

Bucks renew their primary scrapes around doe concentration areas after a snowstorm or heavy rain. JOHN DZIZA

I bagged this buck after a four-inch snowfall moved out of the area.

season progresses, they switch to more browse, especially if there is snow cover. Whitetails favor trees with less tannin, which is acidic. Oak and pine are very acidic, but beech and white cedar are good browse.

During large snowstorms in the North or heavy rainstorms in the South, especially those accompanied by high wind, whitetail movements and locations can be very predictable. This allows a radical bowhunter to pattern them and get in a position to bag a good buck. Typically, the white-tailed deer's home range is one to three miles in size. Within this home range, the deer will follow the same patterns and frequent the same locations during every storm. Once you learn these specific locations, you will find the deer there storm after storm, season after season. Deer seek out the densest cover in the area. Dense bedding cover, such as ever-

TIPS FOR HUNTING BY THE WEATHER

- Keep accurate records of the weather in your hunting area.
- Barometric pressure that is on the rise, or holding at high, is usually an indication of best deer activity.
- Generally, the warmer the weather, the less daytime activity.
- Gusty, swirling winds confuse whitetails, so they hunker down.
- The optimal weather conditions for a radical bowhunter are heavy ground fog or a light, misty rain.
- Radical bowhunters find an advantage hunting immediately after a heavy snowstorm or a rain.

greens with thick understory, provides great shelter from the elements. The vegetation that lines the area is also important.

This radical bowhunter has discovered that when the deer don't come to you, you must go to them. Difficult weather conditions offer the prime time to "go to them." Storms help conceal your movements and cover any noise you make while you move through the area. Move very slowly and be constantly on the alert and ready for a shot, because that big buck you are hoping for could be bedded down just beyond the next tree. Do not look for the entire animal; instead, train your eyes to watch for deer parts and movement.

Fast-moving frontal systems usually leave as quickly as they arrived, especially during the early season. Whitetails will stay in the security of the dense cover until the storm has passed. After leaving the protection of the heavy cover, the hungry deer will ransack a nearby food source. If you saw deer in a feeding area before the storm, go back to the same location, because they will return there as long as they were not spooked.

Storms that were triggered by a front are often followed by frigid arctic air. It is common to experience bitterly cold weather just after the front passes. In most cases, this windy, frigid weather delays the deer from leaving the protection and security of their bedding areas. If you are bowhunting on a day like this, continue to hunt in these protected areas until the weather conditions improve and the deer move out to feed.

After many years of studying and bowhunting white-tailed deer, I have concluded that one of the best times to be hunting trophy bucks is immediately after a snowstorm or heavy rain. The data I have collected over the years has shown a dramatic increase in deer activity at those times, and I have put tags on several really good bucks just after these frontal systems have moved out of the areas I was hunting.

CHAPTER 7

Late-Season Tactics

During the late season, a radical bowhunter always plans to hunt a favorite hot spot. Thanks to the second rut and the fact that big bucks are desperate to replace lost body fat before winter, late-season hunts can offer some exceptional opportunities. There are outstanding prospects for the bowhunter who has the time and patience to persist. Let's face it—some of us just can't get enough of bowhunting for big whitetail bucks. We are constantly looking for ways to extend our hunting pleasure, whether in the last days of the season or in our memories as we relive a truly golden hunt.

> The buck picked his way slowly through the leafless branches, stopping now and then to sniff for the scent of man or other predator. As I sat in my stand during the last week of hunting season, I realized that this guy probably was a vestige from the gun-hunting season. As the rifle hunters left the woods and even the most avid bowhunters either bagged their kills or gave up, this fellow began making his usual rounds again . . .

Many states have extended bowhunting seasons, and the prerut and peak-rut phases give way to a late-season rut commonly called the second rut. Hunting at this time can be a challenging yet effective way to bag your buck if your earlier efforts have left your tag unfilled.

The late-season rut offers a second chance for bucks to breed does that were not caught or did not conceive during the peak of the first rut, as well as does born late in the year, whose biological clocks are just a bit behind. It also offers a second chance for the bowhunter to get out in the deer woods again before winter kicks into full gear.

As a buck senses a lessening of pressure and receives chemical signals from hot does, he'll begin moving about during daylight hours in his quest to find a receptive female. When bowhunting the second rut, it is important that you know where the doe family units are hanging out,

Bucks return and renew their scrapes just before the second rut. Keep those Ultimate Drippers going and your scouting cameras loaded.

WILDLIFE RESEARCH CENTER

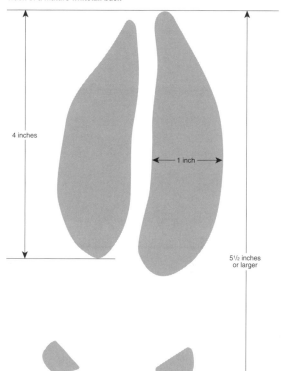

Track of a mature whitetail buck. Notice the width and look for the dew claws.

because the young does that were born that year are still part of the family unit. It may be difficult to determine when the second rut is starting in your area without knowing where the girls are feeding and bedding. Only about 25 percent of those young fawns will even come into an estrous cycle at this time.

When scouting during the late season, look for fresh sign. December rubs or scrapes may mean that a buck is on the trail of a doe coming into a late estrus. Such sign is an indication that he still inhabits the area. If there is fresh snow, scrapes will stand out noticeably against the white backdrop. New rubs will look raw against tree bark that is wet from a winter storm. Keep alert for scrapes or rubs that are only a few days old.

Try hunting a little higher, and pick out a tree that has plenty of background to keep you from being silhouetted against the sky. The best method for bowhunting this second rut period is to hang close to the well-traveled corridors between the feeding and bedding areas. Look closely for a secondary trail with large tracks in the ground or snow. The track should be at least five and a half inches long from the tip to the dew

Late-season buck bagged outside his bedroom door. Notice the camo; a radical bowhunter makes use of the proper gear in any situation.

claw, the hoof at least four inches long, and half of the hoof at least one inch wide. There should also be signs of new rubs and scrapes along the trail. A couple really nice bucks I harvested during this time of the season would not travel the well-worn trails the rest of the deer were using. Instead, they took their own secondary routes, which offered much more cover for protection. Both of these mature bucks were in areas with a lot of hunting pressure, and they repatterned and avoided their usual routes.

Dwindling food supplies will force the deer to feed later in the mornings and earlier in the afternoons. If a buck has found a late-season larder, he'll visit often to fill up as other crops are consumed or disappear. Acorns from white and red oaks, beechnuts, and persimmons may attract whitetail bucks at this time of year. Agricultural fields of winter wheat will attract deer in the late fall and early winter. The old adage "find the food and you have found the deer" is especially true at this time of the season. Because of the unavailability of some crops or food sources, and the fact that snow may hide even more, you need to know what late-season foods exist in your hunting area.

Rubs like this are made by very mature bucks.

Another late-season tactic is to find a buck's bedding area and set up your treestand or ground blind nearby. When a certain amount of hunting pressure is applied, mature whitetail bucks become virtually nocturnal. The fact is, it doesn't take a lot of pressure to push these old bruisers underground. In reality, they probably are not totally nocturnal. But these mature bucks, which have been conditioned to avoid hunting pressure over several seasons, will take refuge in their bedding areas right after dawn and may not leave until just before dusk. Thus it's critical to set up your ambush nearby to take advantage of this tendency. Stick by them in the early dawn and late afternoon, when a buck may travel to or from them before or after eating.

Several years ago, my work schedule forced me to miss opening week of bow season in my home state. I feared that too many hunters tramping through the woods would leave me high and dry. So I decided to wait out week two until the woods thinned out a bit, then try my luck again. Well, my work schedule necessitated traveling most of the fall, hunting in different locations, and demanded that I forgo my last week of domestic bowhunting. I was sorely disappointed.

Not wanting to miss a season, I decided to hunt a neighboring state that offered a later season. Some willy-nilly scouting revealed some fresh scrapes. Then I meticulously picked my way around this area until I thought I had found a potentially productive bedding area. It was in a perfect location on a southwest exposure in very dense cover. There were several fresh rubs on trees, and a few of the trees had bases the size of telephone poles. More serious scouting paid off as I caught a glimpse of a set of heavy antlers heading into the bedding area early one morning. That was enough for me to decide to try my luck at bagging this big guy by positioning a treestand on a well-worn trail on the fringe of the bedding area.

The ground had a couple inches of snow on it. I sat perched on my stand in that tree, like a hawk on a branch waiting for something to show itself so he could make the move. I was hoping my trophy with the heavy rack would leave his bedding area to go eat or stretch his legs. The only spot where I could place my treestand had me facing directly into the sunset—not an enviable position, and one I try to avoid. Between the snow and the sunset, I would have been severely visually handicapped were it not for a good pair of polarized sunglasses. Sunglasses can be an effective tool to add to your bag of tricks, but make sure you invest in a quality pair. Some are effective, but others just darken glare.

So there I sat waiting, watching, trying not to stare into the fireball of the setting sun. Well, the glasses and the strategy paid off. When I heard

Fresh snow softens your footsteps as you move slowly to your stand location.
JOHN DZIZA

Whitetail bucks renew scrapes just outside their bedding areas during the late season. A radical bowhunter looks for fresh sign. JOHN DZIZA

some branches rustling, I turned my head slowly to the left and looked into my DeerView Mirror. This device is similar to a car's rearview mirror, allowing you to see behind you without spooking an approaching buck by moving your head. I could see the reflection of Mr. Big picking his way toward a well-used travel lane.

He did not present me with a good shot that day, but I knew I was in the right place and that we would meet again. And had I not ventured into those December woods, I would not have had that late-season opportunity. A radical bowhunter takes advantage of any hunting experience that can enhance and prolong hunting pleasure. Extending my season with late-fall and early-winter bowhunting is terrific, and I am envious of those who live in states that offer such liberal bow seasons.

Hunting these late-season bucks can be quite different from hunting at other times, and you may have to adjust for such things as moon phases, weather, and hunter intervention. There may also be some advantages. You may be able to access some areas you can't even get to during the regular season. A swamp that is frozen over is much easier to cross than when it is wet and you are knee-deep in mud. A fresh, dry snow can silence your footsteps as you walk, and you will be amazed at how close you can get to a buck by slow stalking.

In some areas, the stress of the primary rut, intense weather, and low food availability can result in bucks shedding their antlers during the late season. This can be a productive time to find a good shed, and it means there will be a buck you can match wits with next season. JOHN DZIZA

It is especially critical that you eliminate your human scent at this time of season. These bucks have been scenting hunters all season, and they will do everything in their power to stay clear of you by avoiding your surrounding area. If they smell you, they will work right around you without your even knowing they were there.

Use your time wisely, and enjoy your season by taking advantage of all the hunting days available to you. If you don't get a buck on opening day, don't despair: there is still some great hunting even into December.

If you live in or near a state that offers such a generous season, plan to hunt the late season next year. One of these late-season trips to the deer woods could end up being some of the best days you'll spend bowhunting. Besides, how else can you justify spending all that money every year on new bowhunting gear unless you get a lot of use out of it?

PART THREE

HOW:

Use the radical bowhunter approach to setting up

.

CHAPTER 8

Scouting and Hunting from the Fringes

Big bucks don't get that way by being dumb or by being easy to hunt. Make a mistake while hunting a big buck, and your chances of bagging him may be gone. The weekend bowhunter goes in for the kill each and every time out. The weekend bowhunter uses the shotgun approach, figuring the more time he spends in the lair of the trophy, the better his odds. The weekend bowhunter assumes that a big buck forgets. The weekend bowhunter rarely bags the big buck.

The radical bowhunter knows that it takes only one golden opportunity to bag a trophy buck. The radical bowhunter knows that it's better to wait for the optimal situation to create an opportunity. The radical bowhunter knows that blowing it even once may end the season because the biggest, most elusive whitetail bucks will not make the same mistake twice. Time in the woods is important, but the more time you spend preparing for that golden opportunity, the better your odds. That's why sometimes it's a better strategy to spend time on the fringes of your prime hunting area—before *and* during the season—before you go in for the kill.

As we covered earlier in the book, your first challenge is finding a big buck. This effort should not start on opening day or even in the few weeks prior. Begin scouting right after the season, while big bucks still sport antlers, and in the spring after the snow has melted and before the foliage reappears. I like to deploy my scouting cameras right after the hunting season. (Refer to chapter 9 for a detailed discussion of scouting cameras.) There is no better way to learn which deer are still around. With hunting pressure gone, few if any people in the woods, and temperatures dipping to the point that deer need more food, the postseason search for Mr. Big can be especially fruitful if you concentrate around food sources. And if you find a big buck this time of year, you have a lot of time to learn his ways and determine his boundaries before the next hunting season.

Advantageous placement of scent drippers and cameras can get you some fantastic photos and perhaps evidence of a mature buck that survived hunting season. WILDLIFE RESEARCH CENTER

After the snow melts, walk the woods looking for scrape lines, rub lines, bedding areas, and other sign. You don't dare traipse through those areas during the season, so take advantage of the off-season to walk every bit of the area you can hunt. You'll be amazed at how well snow cover has preserved scrapes and other sign. And you never know when you might stumble on a big shed antler, another good clue as to the whereabouts of Mr. Big.

SCOUTING FOR EARLY-SEASON SPOTS
In addition to postseason and springtime scouting, do some additional scouting in the weeks leading up to opening day. Your goal now should be to determine the optimal spot for an early-season ambush. Again aided by scouting cameras, you want to find a chink in the big buck's armor, such as a predictable location near which he tends to head back to a bedding area in the early morning or a where he tends to pass in search of an evening meal. Summer, with its bugs and heavy foliage, usually sees few

A shed like this nice five-pointer indicates that the buck is still roaming the woods. He will follow the same patterns next fall. Get ready radical bowhunters. JOHN DZIZA

people in the woods. Deer, therefore, frequently expose themselves during daylight this time of year, especially early and late in the day.

Many years ago, I scouted a new hunting spot for the first time. (This was way before scouting cameras. It was even before scouting was fashionable!) I put up a treestand overlooking a couple of fields from a distance, one planted with corn, the other with alfalfa. I put the treestand really high, because I knew the mosquitoes would be fierce. It was late August and the evening was perfect. I had been in my stand for only a short while when two magnificent ten-pointers emerged into the alfalfa, both with antlers still covered in velvet. I was hundreds of yards away, on the opposite side of the fields from where I knew any deer would emerge, and there was a state highway just seventy-five yards behind me. I watched these two bucks intently with my binoculars to see where they would go so I'd know where to set up an opening-day stand. Pretty soon the field was full of deer. I found it remarkable that the two big bucks had come out first.

Early-season photos can help you hone in on a buck. Place your cameras in predictable locations, and when bucks are returning to their bedding areas in the early morning, you'll have the proof that they are around.
WILDLIFE RESEARCH CENTER

Don't be in a hurry to leave your stand. Staying until dark and the deer have left the area will ensure that you do not spook them or blow your ambush site.

JOHN DZIZA

Amazingly, those two bucks gradually fed their way right up to me along the edge of the corn, which I suspect provided them with cover and a sense of security. The area between the highway and me was dense woods, so the traffic didn't seem to faze the deer. Those deer parked themselves in that corner by my stand, so I got stuck waiting until after dark to climb down.

After a nearly identical experience the next night, I left my stand in place but moved to a different observation point for the weeks prior to opening day. More often than not, those two ten-point bucks ended up within shooting range of my stand.

Opening day came and I was in my stand that afternoon, fighting mosquitoes. The weather was ideal, and I had already decided which of the two ten-pointers I was going to take. What I didn't anticipate was the parade of other bowhunters who apparently also had permission to hunt this property. They all went where I would have gone had I not scouted:

on the edge of the woods across the field where the deer had come out. I never saw those bucks again. In the process, I learned some important lessons, both about deer behavior and how I needed to prepare for my hunt—especially that I needed to be more inquisitive with landowners when securing permission! I never dreamed other hunters would waylay the golden opportunity I had created.

RUT SPOTS ON THE FRINGE

Scouting for early-season spots is one thing; scouting for rut spots is another. Once the prerut is under way, the radical bowhunter spends some time on the fringe watching for where the deer like to move before he ever starts hunting. This during-the-season-scouting is much like duck hunting. Some of my best duck hunts were the product of first sitting and watching where the ducks *wanted* to land—which is rarely the same as where it *looks* like they might want to land.

While scouting in Iowa, I was scoping out a field surrounded by woods with a small cornfield food plot on the south perimeter. I set up my ground blind up at one end of the corn and kicked back to observe. If Mr. Big showed up, I hoped to be able to coax him close with my grunt call or rattling antlers. He never did appear, but over the next several days, I watched lots of other nice bucks. Many of them either entered or exited the field from the north, using an obscure trail that I had never seen them use before. It got to be a routine. So I moved a stand to that trail and during the rut had a ball watching Pope & Young bucks travel close by. No, Mr. Big never showed, but I felt that I was in the right spot in case he did.

Hunting on the fringe of an area offers one critical advantage: Getting to and from it does not disrupt deer activity. The weekend bowhunter picks a very specific spot in the midst of the cover, hoping a shooter buck comes within twenty-five to thirty yards. The radical bowhunter hunts from the fringe, hoping to see a big buck within hearing distance so he can be coaxed over. Obviously, it's a whole lot easier to get within two hundred yards than twenty yards, especially when you haven't walked through the buck's bedroom.

Years ago, I would have called working the fringe scouting and wouldn't have known how to turn it into a hunting opportunity if the situation was right. Today, using grunt calls and rattling antlers, you can call a buck and never risk disrupting deer activity.

PICKING YOUR SPOT ON THE FRINGE

When selecting a fringe spot, keep two things in mind: sight lines and wind direction. The most important issue is sight lines and your ability to see the surrounding territory. Try to set up on a hill overlooking a valley

Rattling and calling from fringe locations is a very productive technique used by the radical bowhunter. JOHN DZIZA

whenever possible. A good vantage point is crucial—it's the whole point. That said, the higher and farther away you are from prime deer travel paths, the more difficult it will be to call a big buck up to you.

To successfully deal with wind direction, have several predetermined fringe spots where you know you won't spook deer visually and you can walk in and out without bumping them. Then, depending on the wind the day you're hunting, you can make a quick decision on where to go to keep yourself downwind from the deer. One of the beauties of hunting from a fringe spot is that if the wind direction shifts, you can move to one of your other locations without ruining the hunting.

A ground blind is usually your best option for hunting fringe locations. It is simpler and quieter to setup than a treestand and it is easier to move so that you can quickly modify a setup. Ground blinds can also be set up in areas that have little cover. Cover keeps the deer from seeing you, but it also keeps you from seeing the deer. Also, you can sit much longer in a blind simply because you can move around without being seen. I've frequently spent entire days in a blind, something I dread in a treestand. Still, I have hunted the fringes from a treestand, especially when ten to fifteen feet gives me a superior vantage point. There are also times when I'll use neither—but getting a shot while ground standing is tricky.

SCOUTING *AND* HUNTING

If a big buck shows himself while you're on a fringe spot, assess the situation before taking any action. Consider what he might do and whether or not you think the time is right to coax him over. Tell yourself that your first priority is scouting. That said, if he makes a move that makes him vulnerable, be prepared for it. Your setup should be perfect, your decoy deployed, and your arrow knocked. Never go afield during hunting season without the express intent of making it happen.

When do you go in for the kill? Hunting the fringe is safe and it can be very protective. There are times when I never leave the fringe. Based on the fringe spot location, your proximity to the deer, and the likelihood you can coax a big buck within shooting range, you may prefer to stay on the fringe and wait for the right opportunity. In other cases, the fringe is merely an interim spot from which you can watch and wait to move to a predetermined location without spooking the deer.

The time of the season will also affect your strategy. If it's early season, avoid the fringe and go straight to prime spots, especially on opening day when you're hoping to waylay that big buck while he is most vulnerable. The only reason I wouldn't go in right away would be an unfavorable shift in the weather.

This view from a ground blind shows the clear shots possible from this fringe location. Look closely; a radical bowhunter hedges his bets and in this case has also set up a treestand in case movement is necessary to get in range. JOHN DZIZA

During the season, start on the fringe and move in when you feel you know what the buck is going to do—you've seen enough to pattern him and don't want to chance coaxing him to a less-than-optimal setup.

In the rut, wait on the fringes until things are in full swing, when the big bucks throw caution into the wind. Once this is underway, you want to be in the midst of the activity. Sure, odds of coaxing during this time are good, but the odds of a hot doe trolling a monster past are even better. That's the one thing that really makes the decision easy. When I see a hot doe with a buck on the prowl, I am going in. Unfortunately, too many weekend warriors hunt just morning and evening and miss the middle of the day, which often is the best time to be out.

NO CUTTING CORNERS

When working fringe locations, don't assume that you can get away with a relaxed approach to hunting. Remember that radical bowhunters never cut corners if they are serious about taking a trophy buck. We've all done it—cut corners only to get burned. Remember, you are not hunting an average deer. You are hunting the best deer in the woods. He is big because he is good.

I hunted one Wisconsin brute until the bitter end. The last morning of the season presented me with six inches of fresh snow. I watched this buck move between a piece of woods and a brushy swamp using a finger of cover. There were no trees, and access was difficult. I did everything right and had my ground blind spot predetermined. The wind was non-existent. As I neared my spot, I grew tired of walking through the cover, enduring the snow from overhanging branches falling down my neck. So I cut out of the cover and walked along the very edge.

After a morning of no action, I decided to head back for some lunch. As I retraced my tracks, I noticed deer tracks only fifty yards from my spot. They came out of the woods and went down to the finger of cover and along the edge—right where they were supposed to. Where the deer tracks cut my tracks, they stopped and turned around. A closer look revealed the tracks were extra large, likely from the buck I was hunting. I cut a corner by walking outside the cover and I paid the price.

People always ask me what to do if they've accidentally educated a big buck. I tell them to move to a different area in his territory and not to make the same mistake twice. This is when hunting the fringe is even more important. Sure, some big bucks will come back the next day—but most of them are already dead.

Long ago, I had an experience with a big buck that proved this point. I got a shot at him, but the arrow deflected off a branch and hit the deer

A radical bowhunter employs any method possible that will put him on a good buck, including the use of a ground stand. This is not my favorite tactic, but in this case it's necessary. JOHN DZIZA

going sideways. The broadhead stuck superficially into the deer's side and fell out on his first bound. Convinced that deer would not be back, I got my hunting buddy, who had already filled his tag, to sit in that stand the next morning just to be sure. That buck came back to the same scrape at the exactly the same time the next morning. He apparently had not associated his experience with danger. Unfortunately, my buddy managed to spook the buck, and he never came back again. I know—I was in that spot every morning thereafter until the end of the season.

The frenzy of the rut may be the only time you can get away with a mistake. Blow out a big buck any other time and you very well might have educated him so that he won't make that same mistake again. Bump him while does are in heat and he may be so preoccupied that he could come back by in fifteen minutes.

The bottom line is that you will do well to get one crack at a big buck. Do not blow the chance by bumping that buck while going into your stand. Instead, hunt a fringe area you can easily access with minimal noise and disruption—a fringe area that doubles as a scouting location and just might give you the edge on the trophy buck of your dreams.

CHAPTER 9

Scouting Cameras: How to Hunt Multiple Spots at Once

Scouting is a critical aspect of successful hunts for big bucks, especially if you are serious about trophy bucks and want to harvest them with any kind of consistency. Information on the whereabouts of big bucks and the timing of their movements is extremely valuable. But as much as we'd like to spend most of our time in the woods, it's just not possible for most of us. Instead, a radical bowhunter uses strategically placed scouting cameras to "hunt" multiple spots at once.

The technique is simple: You place the camera where deer are likely to travel, and when one passes by, the camera is automatically triggered to take a picture. A few weeks later, you return, pick up the exposed film, and reload the camera with a fresh roll of film. In the case of a digital camera, it's even easier—you just view the pictures. You can then evaluate at home what the camera has recorded.

A scouting camera serves as a faithful scout that never sleeps. It allows a radical bowhunter to scout while going about all his daily activities miles and miles away. I try to hunt several hot states and provinces each fall, and it's difficult to do it effectively when I live more than a thousand miles away from each of them. Multiple scouting-camera setups enable the investigation of several areas at the same time.

Another advantage is that you are not walking all around the area you plan to hunt later. This avoids spooking and repatterning the bucks with all your movements and human scent. The camera allows you to scout whitetail movements and make your actual hunting time more productive without much impact on your target buck's environment. And let's face it, haven't you always wanted to know what you've been missing when you're not in the woods?

If you scout properly during the year, you can use the actual hunting season strictly to harvest an animal. Scouting cameras are the best way to

When set up properly, scouting cameras can be invaluable tools to a radical bowhunter. They can identify not only the number but also the quality of deer in a given area. WILDLIFE RESEARCH CENTER

gain the knowledge you need to increase your odds of shooting trophy deer. You may learn, like I did, that you've been hunting the wrong areas at the wrong times.

For the last several years, since I began to use scouting cameras, my success rate has been astounding, and my days spent hunting per harvested animal drastically decreased. Several friends still kid me about one hunt about ten years ago that was the longest of my life. It was back before I started using a scouting camera. I spent twenty-three days hunting that big buck in southern Iowa before harvesting him. Most guys don't have that much time to hunt and would have had to give up and go home. My wife kept getting those "but Honey" phone calls and figured if I was that obsessed, I might as well get it out of my system. If only I'd had a scouting camera back then!

Much of my time deer hunting has been on unmanaged public land that I've had to share with dozens of other hunters. You may also use this type of hunting habitat.

WHERE AND WHEN TO PLACE CAMERAS

To find good locations to set up scouting cameras, first study topographical maps of the area you are planning to hunt. Look for the kinds of features that attract deer or influence their movement patterns, then go out and scout these areas. If possible, check them out in the early spring immediately after the snow melts, before the forest floor starts to green up. Look for deer trails along the edges of swamps or ridges, rubs, and scrapes.

The ideal trail will look as if it has been there for generations. It will be well-worn, deeply rutted, and on the edge of a bedding area. At this point, you are not looking for lots of deer prints. Trails typically have the most activity during the two to three weeks of the rut, but the rest of the year, deer traffic on them is minimal. These trails are used by bucks to travel quickly through does' home ranges, going from one family unit to another in search of estrous does. Using my trusty scouting cameras, I have discovered that typically if one buck is using these trails, others are too. It seems that where the dominant buck goes, subordinates follow. Several bucks have been photographed using these trails from season to season.

Once you identify areas that show deer activity, record them on your maps and global positioning system (GPS) unit. Then forget about them until the fall. In early October, pull out your maps, reanalyze the locations, and put scouting cameras at the best ones. Place your cameras about a month before the rut starts, and leave them set up for at least a month in the same location—in most cases until the rut is over—in order

This is the third buck caught on camera at this location in a week's time. Scouting cameras accurately date-time stamp their shots. WILDLIFE RESEARCH CENTER

This great shot of a great buck was caught on film by a scouting camera set up just off a feed area, where a scent wick was placed. WILDLIFE RESEARCH CENTER

to properly determine a trail's potential. You may see little or no buck activity for the first few weeks, but when the rut starts to pick up, it will increase quickly. Never give up on a location until the rut is over. Last year's results have little bearing on what to expect this year. A trail that was full of bucks one year may have none the next. Identify as many likely looking locations as possible, and put out as many scouting cameras as you can afford or have time for.

Don't be alarmed if you get only one photograph of a particular buck. It does not mean he has been spooked, gone nocturnal, or left the area completely. It just means you got only one photograph of that buck. Chances are he is still in the area but did not walk in front of the camera lens again. Over many years, this radical bowhunter has observed that bucks seldom walk in the same exact spot twice. They may use the same travel corridor, but they wander over a path that can be fifty yards wide or more, making it difficult to photograph them multiple times. So if you get a photograph of a good buck, you can usually assume he will be in that area again. Keep an accurate log of all the bucks you capture with your camera at these prospective setup locations.

Typically, about 70 percent of all the photographs I get with my scouting cameras are at night. Yet many times I also see these bucks I've photographed at night during legal hunting hours. I think this is because during darkness, deer are more likely to walk on the well-defined trails,

Taking a nontraditional view, a radical bowhunter makes use of the latest technology to locate his buck. This big buck was harvested just four days after he was shot by the scouting camera.

which are where I usually set up my scouting cameras. In the daylight, with better visibility, the bucks move off the well-used paths along travel corridors spanning these trails.

Hunters often describe coming across an unbelievable spot with more deer sign than they have ever seen before. The trail was like a cowpath through a field, deep and rutted with tracks. They set up a few treestands and maybe a ground blind, sat there for several whole days, but never saw a deer. If they had used scouting cameras, they could have saved themselves a lot of time and effort, because such spots usually are all-night traffic areas. Where they should have set up was at the closest area of heavy cover downwind from the trail.

Once I capture a buck with one of my scouting cameras, I get in there and hunt as soon as possible. I like to hunt these spots both morning and evening for at least two or three days, sitting there all day from dark to dark. This goes completely against conventional wisdom, which warns about hunting the same spot every day. But my scouting cameras have shown me that bucks seldom return to the same area every day, so I wait on my stand until the buck comes back. A few years ago, I got a picture of a nice heavy-racked, forked-brow-tined buck in Missouri on a Tuesday and put an arrow through him on Saturday evening, after having hunted my stand for four solid days.

Getting a picture of one of those big bruisers can give you the patience you need to score. Odds are that if he was there once, he will be back again. If you don't see the deer after a few days, reevaluate your decision and move if you feel it is warranted. Keep your scouting cameras out and look for changes in deer movements or the sudden appearance of a good buck.

CHOOSING A CAMERA

A scouting camera is, without a doubt, the best means to scout deer. A scouting camera allows the hunter to determine where and when deer are moving and the quality and trophy potential of the deer in the area. They allow the hunter to scout twenty-four hours a day, 365 days a year, with minimal intrusion on the deer's range. A scouting camera is the most vital piece of equipment in a radical bowhunter's hunting arsenal. I say this for a simple reason: The best equipment in the world won't make up for hunting the wrong location. With a scouting camera, you can ensure that you are hunting the best locations.

Key Features

The key features or requirements you should be looking for when you are ready to purchase a scouting camera include the following:

- *Long battery life.* This is essential—you don't want to intrude upon these areas every week. In addition to having a longer operating time, longer battery life also equates to lower operating cost. With some cameras, battery cost can quickly surpass the initial cost of your camera. You want a unit that can be left unattended for at least thirty days. A scouting camera that uses batteries inefficiently may end up in the field with dead batteries, providing no benefit to the hunter.
- *Versatile range of camera delays.* This is the time between photos taken when a camera is triggered. Set short camera delays when

Quality camera, quality buck. This wall-hanger was visiting a mock scrape when the DeerCam captured him. WILDLIFE RESEARCH CENTER

Don't miss your shot with either your camera or your bow. DeerCam cameras, when properly used, will give you fewer blank photos than the less expensive models. As with most things, you get what you pay for.

you use your scouting cameras on a trail—fifteen to thirty seconds is ideal to ensure that you photograph every deer on that trail. On scrapes, use longer delays of five to ten minutes.

- *High quality.* The main component of a scouting camera is, of course, the camera. Scouting packages with name-brand, high-quality cameras have the advantage of better images, more powerful flash performance, and better reliability.

Cost

Price of a film unit ranges from less than $100 to $300. But over time, you will spend more on operating costs—film, development, and batteries—than the initial cost of the unit. Operating costs include wasted film resulting from blank, nonanimal photographs. Each film photograph costs about 25 to 35 cents. If a camera generates a lot of erroneous photographs, operating cost can get excessive. Though no scouting camera can guarantee that every photograph will have an animal in it, the better units will produce far fewer blank photos.

The more expensive models from each company use name-brand cameras that have much lower operating costs and more rugged, weatherproof lockable enclosures. Inexpensive units use no-name cameras that have higher operating costs and less durable enclosures. Though both types may operate adequately, the more expensive scouting cameras will be much more reliable, take better-quality photographs, and have much lower operating costs. So over time, you will end up saving money purchasing a quality unit. Of the many full-featured film cameras available, CamTracker and DeerCam lead the pack. But feature for feature and dollar for dollar, DeerCam would be my first choice every time.

Digital Cameras

Digital units cost from $300 to more than $1,000. Digital scouting cameras have one big advantage over film scouting cameras: You can see the images in the field. This can make a huge difference in real-world scouting and hunting when you want to respond quickly. Waiting for film processing can result in a missed opportunity.

Digital cameras, though pricier up front, deserve special consideration. With no film to purchase or develop, operating costs can be substantially reduced. True operating costs need to be evaluated carefully, however. Some digital scouting cameras require a lot of batteries, which can be very expensive. The best digital units may operate for months on a single set of batteries, giving them an overall cost far less than that of a film camera. In addition, the digital units are not restricted by film roll size; they can take hundreds of images, providing the hunter with considerably more information.

The best digital scouting cameras use a custom-designed mechanism that is optimized for scouting-camera use. These cameras have been optimized for battery life, flash performance, lens selection, and image quality at a lower overall cost. Most commercial digital cameras are designed for general use, where power consumption and flash performance is less critical. Of all the units I have tried and tested, the Cuddeback Digital scouting camera is my hands-down, number-one pick because of its quality components, ease of operation, and price. CamTracker, Highlander Sports, and Trail Sense Engineering also make quality digital units.

The most frequently asked question about using a scouting camera is whether the flash spooks deer. Mark Cuddeback has made an interesting observation. He has been using scouting cameras for more than fifteen years and is convinced that the camera does not alter deer behavior. The sound of the camera as it focuses and opens the shutter does get the deer's attention, however; this can be seen in the photographs that show the deer looking at the camera. The first thing he noticed when he started using his new digital scouting camera was the completely relaxed look of the deer in his images, exhibiting a more natural and completely

This buck is relaxed and unaware that he's posing for a shot taken by a Cuddeback digital scouting camera. WILDLIFE RESEARCH CENTER

unalarmed demeanor. I think it is safe to say that the quiet operation of the digital cameras is less likely to alarm deer.

Even with all their advantages, digital cameras are not for everyone. They require a little more technical knowledge and have a longer learning curve. Users should own a personal computer so they can archive, view, and print images. For those who prefer supereasy operation, film cameras are the best choice. But the hunter who is willing to put in the effort to learn to use a digital camera will be rewarded with instant images and lower overall long-term cost.

THE RADICAL BOWHUNTER'S METHOD FOR SCOUTING-CAMERA SUCCESS

My friend Ron Bice of Wildlife Research Products and I have taken thousands of photographs each year over the last several years. We have found that using this method to set up our scouting cameras produces the best results:

- Set up your scouting camera while the deer are not in the bedding area. You will get photographs of bucks during daylight hours when they can be hunted.

A scouting camera set up properly outside a buck's bedding area will provide photos of daylight activity. That translates into a great spot to hang a treestand or erect a ground blind. WILDLIFE RESEARCH CENTER

- Slip in and out without detection. You don't want to let the deer know a human predator has been there. Make sure you are completely scent-free by showering and shampooing beforehand with unscented soaps and wearing a Scent-Lok suit and rubber boots and gloves.
- Keep your unit in a plastic container with dry foliage from the area you plan to hunt. Important: Do not use wet foliage in the container, because the dampness will affect the function of your camera over time. Also consider carrying your unit in a Scent-Lok daypack, which will remove much of the foreign odor.
- Set up a scent dispenser five feet off the ground with a curiosity lure such as Trails End 307.
- Mount your unit approximately twelve feet on average from the scent dispenser. Never set up beyond forty feet if you want to be able to determine the quality of animals in your area. The top of the unit should be mounted to a tree $3^{1}/_{2}$ feet from the ground and level.

Make sure to set the timing between exposures properly for the location. You want a longer interval between shots at mock scrapes than on a trail. This helps prevent multiple photos of one buck and saves film for more effective use. On a trail, you can shorten the interval because a buck will quickly move out of the area and go on his way.

Spray your scouting camera housing and the host tree with Scent Killer to eliminate any human odor.

Always wear rubber gloves when setting up or handling your scouting camera to avoid contaminating it with your scent. Use gloves thin enough to let you work the camera, settings, buttons, and clamp.

- Spray the enclosure and cords with Autumn Formula Scent Killer, covering the lens opening with your rubber-gloved finger.
- Follow the same procedures to reload your unit with film every two weeks (not required for a digital unit). Do not run in to check it every few days in your excitement to see what you have, or you could blow your cover. Be patient.

CHAPTER 10

The Importance of Keeping Quiet

Since I started bowhunting many years ago, I have learned some hard lessons. A white-tailed deer will not hang around if it hears any noises that are unnatural. A radical bowhunter knows that keeping quiet is imperative if you want to bag the really big bucks. Nowhere is silence—sweet, sweet silence—more important than in your treestand or ground blind during bowhunting season. As a matter of fact, it becomes a critical factor in hunting long before you arrive at the spot you are going to hunt for the day. It begins the moment you arrive at your hunting place and park your vehicle.

Noise may well be the primary cause of most lost trophy opportunities. Slamming that car door can have the same disastrous results as someone shouting to you while you sit in your stand or blind. A whitetail buck is so in tune with his environment that even the slightest foreign noise can alert him, and the only sound the bowhunter may hear is the swish of that white tail as it waves "au revoir."

Achieving and maintaining a quiet bowhunting session involves numerous factors, many of which are easy to control, and all of which are important. To hunt silently as a radical bowhunter, you must deaden the sounds from your equipment and clothing and prepare your hunting locations during the preseason. Enter the woods on the opening day of bowhunting season with an awareness of the sounds you make and hear in the woods, making a conscious effort to move quietly and remain as silent as possible.

Start by thinking about what causes noise. You are responsible for the noise you create. Not only must you learn to move quietly, but stifling a sneeze or subduing a cough can be critical as well. In order to lower the volume and amounts of sound made in the woods, you also must silence your clothing and every piece of equipment you bring with you, including your bow, accessories, backpack, and treestand or ground blind.

Stalking as you approach and exit your hunting location is critical. Walking slowly and watching where each foot is placed can eliminate brushing sounds or snapped twigs and branches. Try to choose paths that allow you to walk old logging roads, dry creekbeds, or soft, muddy spots. Avoid walking on dry, crackly leaves or brittle twigs. This radical bowhunter has even gone so far as to enter the woods before the season begins to clear leaves and debris from the ground with a rake along paths I plan to use. Preseason planning can allow you to remove branches that might hinder a quiet approach, and checking the area around your stand—including the shooting lane—to identify offending branches or limbs can pay dividends during the hunting season.

Once you have arrived at your hunting location, quietly scrape any residue from your hunting boots with a stick so that a mud or ice bomb will not drop through the grate of your treestand at the worst possible moment. If you use a portable treestand, carry a square of carpet to quiet your floor space as well as help keep your feet warmer.

A stand that can be erected and used quietly is important. From my experience, climbing stands are noisier than portable treestands. Testing your stand or ground blind at home and silencing it as much as possible before entering the woods is a good idea. Spray all the moving parts of the stand with dry film lubricant. Once it dries there is no odor, and it keeps moving parts well-lubricated and very quiet. Duct tape can be used at metallic contact points to deaden noise.

Erect your stand a few days prior to hunting season. Once you have it in place, test it again for any squeaks. Sit in the stand and listen for any kind of noise as you shift your body weight and twist from side to side. Try drawing your bow from the stand in every possible position and angle to see if anything connected with the treestand has any little squeak.

Once the first day of the season arrives, portable treestand users should carry a Therm-A-Mat and strap it at the base of the stand to quiet any foot movement; it will also keep your feet warm. Safety harnesses must be used without banging or clanging together. My favorite is the Fall Guy harness system, which I think is the safest treestand safety system available. It was designed by automotive engineers using safety belt retractors that protect you not only in your stand but also when climbing in or out of the stand.

Erecting a treestand on hunting day is definitely not a good idea, but I have seen many bowhunters do it. A ground blind generally is much quieter to put up and take down, so you could put one up the day of the hunt. This goes against the policy of being completely set up in advance, but it may be necessary if you are hunting on public land and you fear your ground blind may not be there the next day. Make your setup and takedown as quiet and unobtrusive as possible.

Ground blinds are quieter to hunt from, especially on a very cold day or during inclement weather. Maintaining silence and keeping still when perched in a treestand are not easy to master, though they can be done. That is why I would rather hunt at eye level out of a ground blind, especially as the season progresses and the temperature drops.

Silencing your bow is one of the most important considerations. With a recurve or longbow, this is relatively simple, but silencing a compound requires much more effort. A traditional bow needs little more than a string silencer and a padded arrow rest to ensure a silent firing, but it requires some effort to keep the mechanical noises generated by the wheels and pulleys of a compound bow from spooking the buck of your dreams.

Three different noises are produced by a compound bow, and they occur at three different stages of its use. When the bowstring is pulled to full draw, it creates squeaks and creaks and friction noises along the cable guard and arrow rest. Other noises occur as the bow is released. Vibrations after the arrow clears the bow produce noises as well. Before working on silencing a compound bow, it might be a good idea to first consider investing in a new, quiet bow. For the last six years, I have been shooting a Mathews bow, which has many innovations that keep it quiet. Plus, these bows fire like lightning and are a pleasure to shoot. But if you can't afford a new bow or think of parting with one that shoots great, silencing a compound bow is not all that difficult if you approach it systematically, one step at a time.

First inspect and shoot your bow to determine what kinds of noises are being created and where they are being produced. Squeaky eccentric wheels are a common problem; they can be silenced with a bit of vegetable oil applied to the wheels' axles or string channels.

Having a silent arrow rest is critical. A good friend of mine was hunting in Saskatchewan a few years ago and sat for five days waiting for a shot opportunity at this really fantastic buck that he figured would have a Pope and Young score in the high 160s. It was an extremely cold morning when the buck showed himself, and he was picture perfect. My buddy drew his bow a little early and held at full draw, waiting for the buck to come into his shooting lane. As luck would have it, the buck stopped for what seemed like an hour. Have you ever pulled your string and tried to hold it while those moments seemed to crawl by? Well, that's what happened—not really a lot of time, but long enough for him to begin having trouble holding the bow at full draw. Finally he had to let down, and when the bow hit bottom, the arrow jumped off the rest from the shock, hit the riser of the bow, and made a loud clank that was clearly audible in the crisp morning air. That's all it took to spook that big boy. My friend ended up hunting two extra days in hopes of seeing the buck again, but that deer never crossed his path again. The outfitter told him later that no other hunter even got a glimpse of that buck for the balance of the deer season. So not only did he lose his chance, but no one else got a shot off at this dandy buck either.

The arrow rest itself should be covered with a silencing material, and in addition, the area above and below the rest should be protected. That way, if an arrow slips off the rest, it will not knock on a hard surface and spook any deer in shooting range. To make your rest silent and deadly, use Teflon tape or tubing on the launcher and felt tape to silence the base of the rest.

Once you have adequately silenced the arrow rest, check the slide on the cable guard to ensure that it works silently. Replace the ones the manufacturer installed if they do not function quietly. Also check out the slide in wet weather, as sometimes a wet slide will make noise. Eliminate friction by spraying some silicone on the cable guard.

When the arrow is released, cams and wheels are apt to make their own noise, with cams making more than wheels. A cat whisker silencer or Limb Saver string leech can lessen the sound of the slap. The string leech will not take all of the sound away, but it will reduce the sound by up to 65 percent when you release an arrow from your bow. Stabilizers can also help quiet a noisy bow. After the arrow clears the bow, another vibration noise is sometimes produced; help reduce it by making sure screws are fastened tightly and having vibration dampeners on your bow.

Once you have your bow quiet, check the arrows in your quiver to make sure that no feathers or vanes are touching, which can create noise. Vanes are not as bad when it comes to noise, but arrows with vanes do not fly as well as those with feathers.

You also need to take a radical approach to silencing yourself. All hunting apparel should be made from materials that do not produce sound. Avoid slippery or crackly nylon. Cotton, chamois, fleece, and wool all can provide you with value in performance and quiet comfort in the field. Raingear may become quite noisy when it is exposed to cold temperatures. I like Scent-Lok's Supreme waterproof and breathable series, which keeps me quiet as well as scent-free and dry.

A little preplanning and a great deal of awareness will keep this buck heading right into the ambush site.

The key is to try on your hunting clothes before going into the field. Move about in them and listen—really listen. A few washings may soften and quiet some fabrics, but sometimes the noise they generate is just too much for the up-close-and-personal encounters that bowhunting requires.

Other gear you carry into the woods may also create a noise problem. Grunt calls and binoculars can be silenced by wrapping them with duct tape. This should deaden any noise that may be created should they bang together or hit the bow. I also use rattling antlers and have found that carrying them hung from their cord, inside my hunting coat with one antler under each armpit (much like spreading your fingers under your arm trying to reach an itch on your lower shoulder blade), allows them to be transported safely and quietly through the woods.

A little preplanning and a lot of awareness can help you quiet the noisemakers and allow you to fully enjoy the excitement of bowhunting that trophy buck you are after. Always remember that silence is golden.

CHAPTER 11

Fool the Deer's Nose by Being Scent-Free

Technology has given the radical bowhunter an edge in fooling the nose of the white-tailed deer. Whitetails live in a world of scent, and humans are an olfactory nightmare. Not only do we smell bad, but we smell badly, as we cannot sense these odors because our noses are not keen enough. It is little wonder then that the average bowhunter finds the biological superiority of a whitetail's nose mystifying. In truth, hunters are outnosed by any species they seek to hunt, and prey species like whitetails, with their keen sense of smell, can be a great challenge.

One way to try to bring this into perspective is to think of dogs. For years, I chased around after field-trial beagles whose joy in life was to sniff out cottontail rabbits. A good beagle can follow a cottontail's trail through thick and thin, across water and rocks, all for the pure pleasure of it. And then there's the bloodhound, which can scent a person who has passed a spot nearly twenty-four hours earlier. Talk about a cold scent and a hot nose! For all our wisdom and insight, we can smell neither the bunny nor the human. In this department, we hunters, are virtually unarmed.

The bad news is that there is not much we can do to improve our own sense of smell. The good news is that we can do something about how much scent we leave behind in the woods as we hunt. And there is something we can do to help compensate for the very highly tuned nose of a white-tailed deer. The answer lies in understanding whitetail behavior in relation to how they interpret these scents that fill their world and learning how to use this to your best advantage.

First let's address the topic of how much scent we emit. Here the rules are pretty straightforward. A radical bowhunter must practice being scrupulously clean, use products that eliminate human scent, wear rubber boots while traveling to and from the treestand or blind, and not touch anything in the woods with bare hands.

We have had an advantage at hiding our scent since Scent-Lok Technologies pioneered odor-eliminating clothing technology in 1992. The original Scent-Lok liner, which hunters wore under their favorite camo, began a new level of scent elimination. When the company simplified things by incorporating this product into camouflage outerwear, the response was overwhelming, and most hunters have come to realize that this product really does work and will help them get closer to game while remaining undetected. It has taken the industry by storm, and now this technology is built into much of our hunting clothing and accessories. Only by wearing odor-eliminating garments can bowhunters fully expect successful scent-free hunting.

Several other companies today have products that use the same technology and are licensed under Scent-Lok's patents. They all work, but Scent-Lok still stands out in the crowd because the company continues to work on improving the technology and has made even greater advances in performance with its new ClimaFlex. The fabric is softer, more flexible, and lighter in weight. Combined with an advanced process that actually fuses the carbon between two layers of fabric, it delivers a level of breathability that was previously unattainable in a scent-elimination garment. Scent-Lok ClimaFlex is also treated with a patented moisture-wicking formula that disperses perspiration away from the skin to keep you dry and comfortable. Scent-Lok ClimaFlex also works even better at eliminating scent.

From the very beginning, Scent-Lok has used rigorous testing to establish a critical tolerance level that deer and other game have for human odor before they become alarmed. ClimaFlex exceeds that tolerance level by more than four times, even after twenty washings. Also, a patented chemical barrier process prevents odor containing skin oils from permanently impregnating the ClimaFlex fabric. Recent tests indicate that garments using the Scent-Lok ClimaFlex do not need to be reactivated as often as any previous odor-eliminating clothing, which in turn minimizes the wear from washing and drying. Better yet, it will adsorb (hold molecules of the material surface) scent longer, making it ideal for extended hunting trips where frequent reactivation may be impractical.

Another innovation by Scent-Lok Technologies is BaseSlayers, an activated carbon scent-control garment designed to be worn next to the skin under other activated carbon-based garments in a multilayer system. BaseSlayers adsorb odors caused by the body's production of gas compounds, which are easily detected by white-tailed deer. These garments will make you even more scent-free and lengthen the amount of time needed between reactivations of outer garments.

There are unique problems when trying to measure the amount of odor that is adsorbed by these activated-carbon products. The amount of detectable odor must be accurate in ppm (parts per million) or ppb (parts per billion). These very small amounts require specialized equipment that can measure the amount of gas concentrations involved. Gas chromatography is the best method for measuring the amount of odors or similar chemical agents in a controlled experiment.

Under very controlled lab conditions, samples of several activated carbon fabrics are placed in airtight glass containers. The containers then are injected with various concentrations of EMA (ethyl methyl amine) for a specified amount of time. EMA is chosen for routine testing due to its ease of handling, consistency, and similar chemical nature of body odor. Then the gas is extracted from the jars and the remaining concentration of EMA that is not absorbed by the fabric is measured using gas chromatography. These tests are repeated time after time using various portions of fabric and small to large amounts of EMA. The tests are also performed using fabrics, which have gone through a number of wash-and-dry cycles so that the scent-absorbing characteristics can be measured for the products' durability over a normal lifecycle.

The test data that was received from all the independent laboratories showed that Scent-Lok is still the most odor-absorbing fabric in the hunting market. It was the only fabric that showed excellent odor absorbency after being washed and dried several times.

Your entire system must be activated before your hunt and stored in a sealed bag. Total scent-free hunting is the result of a systematic approach, each step of which is important to your ultimate success in the deer woods. Besides wearing a multilayer scent-adsorbing system, you have to take other precautions to control your scent as well. It is critical that you wear a head cover to prevent scent from coming off your head. Shower first, paying special attention to your hair, which can be a scent wick. Spray your hands, face, hair, backpack, and bow thoroughly with a scent-eliminating product such as Wildlife Research Center's Scent Killer before entering the woods or putting on your Scent-Lok system. A radical bowhunter always does everything in his power to completely eliminate human scent, because he is aware how critical it is to his continued success at bowhunting big bucks. By using these superior high-tech products on stand, you will see more game up close while remaining undetected.

If you use a system with too little carbon, the deer will smell you and spook; use one with too much carbon, and you needlessly sacrifice breathability, comfort, weight, and softness. It's a delicate balance.

Wearing a Scent-Lok Technologies total system and taking all other necessary precautions to eliminate human odors will give you the best chance of avoiding detection by the whitetail's keen nose so you can get a shot at a big buck of your own.

The other way to try to get an edge on the nose of the buck of your dreams is to use attractants or lures that will smell like a hot doe. A good lure will reach out and grab that buck by his nose and bring him right to you. Obviously one must make proper use of these hunting aids, and they are just that, an aid, even the best scent on the market will not be able to compensate for lack of knowledge or errors in the field.

Some of the most common errors hunters make involve being winded by the deer long before they get into range.

When using any of these products you must think like a trapper because in all reality you are trying to bring the animal into desired

This buck was totally oblivious to the hunter sitting in a ground blind ten yards away. Fastidious personal hygiene, proper use of scent elimination products, and clothing such as a Scent-Lok system help you get up close and personal before you let that arrow fly. WILDLIFE RESEARCH CENTER

position for a killing shot without the trap. The answer again is to learn about and understand how scent is distributed and delivered on the wind.

Any hunter who goes into the woods without obtaining information on the wind patterns of the area or understanding how temperature changes and topography affect the wind may as well be wearing a blindfold. Learn the rudiments of air currents and you'll be able to compensate a bit for the nose Mother Nature gave you.

Air can move at a range of speeds, from a barely perceptible breeze to a hurricane force. Strong, steady winds may be easier to gauge because they usually blow in one direction only, whereas gusty winds change velocity and direction often. A lack of wind may allow your scent to pool about you as you sit for hours in your stand. A slight breeze makes for the best hunting.

Using scents and lures in tandem with a strict regime to eliminate your own odor will bring those big guys right to you. This buck was less than fifteen yards from a Double Bull ground blind. WILDLIFE RESEARCH CENTER

Besides moving horizontally, air also moves vertically. These up-and-down movements are called wind thermals, and they are greatly affected by temperature. Warm air rises, and cooler air drops. Hunting high ground in the morning as the warm air rises helps get your scent out of the way. Stay low later, when the cooler evening air keeps wind thermals closer to the ground.

Using an attractant lure product is another way to use a whitetail's keen nose to the bowhunter's advantage. As the tantalizing aroma of the attractant lure frenzies a buck, he can be pulled to you, in a state of lessened awareness, for your final confrontation.

A radical bowhunter needs to realize the overall importance of scent and air movements. By manipulating these factors to your best advantage, you can better go forth into a whitetail's world of scent by camouflaging yourself from the deer's nose.

Fooling a whitetail's keen sense of smell takes time and effort, but the results of being completely scent-free speak for themselves. For a radical bowhunter, it can mean the difference between sighting deer within shooting range and coming home with an empty tag.

SIX STEPS TO SUCCESSFUL SCENT ELIMINATION

1. Before getting dressed, spray hands, boots, and all accessories with scent-eliminating spray to avoid contaminating garments.
2. Remove garments from storage bag and dress in the field.
3. Spray boots thoroughly with scent-eliminating spray.
4. Be sure all equipment is scent-free before entering hunting area.
5. Always use total stealth approaching and leaving the stand area and during the actual hunt.
6. Return all clothing to storage bag after the hunt. Reactivate garments in a dryer after every thirty to forty hours of use.

CHAPTER 12

Let the Big Buck Tell
You Where to Set Up

Most hunters pick a spot to set up based on where they think a big buck will go. A radical bowhunter lets the big buck pick the spot for him. It's really not that difficult to find those special places—spots where the bucks pass by well within bow range, which is somewhere between fifteen and twenty-five yards—but most hunters don't want to invest the time needed to find these locations. There is no easy way or shortcut to consistent success in bowhunting. As in any activity, success takes time and effort.

Many of us know at least one bowhunter who takes a really nice buck nearly every year. Often he bags one early into the season. Maybe some of us are just plain lucky, but a radical bowhunter never relies solely on luck to put that big buck in front of an arrow. He always takes calculated measures before the season starts to greatly increase the odds in his favor. He won't leave that up-close-and-personal encounter with a trophy-class buck to chance. I'm not talking about shooting two-inch groups at thirty yards with your new bow or making sure your scent-free suit is ready to go. Much more important, you need to know exactly what the bucks you plan to hunt will be doing during the season.

Accordingly, it's important to learn as much as possible about the deer in the area you plan to hunt. Spending time in the woods preseason is important, but so are reviewing the details of past hunts and being in the woods postseason preparing for next year. Learning all you can about whitetail behavior and the terrain in which they live can help you achieve consistent success season after season. A radical bowhunter who puts in a lot of time and effort will reap the rewards and enjoy success as he challenges a master of his environment on his own turf. One way this can be accomplished is by putting out as many scouting cameras as possible in locations that looked the most promising from examining aerial photos or

A radical bowhunter would get excited about this rub. The tree is telephone pole size. Just think how wide the buck's rack must have been to get into this tree.

Let the sign tell you where to set up. A spot like this, with large rubs and heavy cover surrounding the area, would be an ideal setup location. JOHN DZIZA

topographic maps and analyzing deer sign in the area. Make it a game to name all these prospective stand locations and pick which ones you think will produce the most or the biggest bucks.

STUDY PAST HUNTING EXPERIENCES

When deciding where to set up for mature bucks, rely on not only the principles of whitetail behavior, but also the specifics of your past hunting experiences, such as trying to figure out where a buck was immediately before he came into your range and what brought him there. This information can help you determine the best possible stand locations for future hunting seasons. Understanding whitetail behavior and movement can help a radical bowhunter have a better chance of getting an opportunity to arrow a big buck by locating the one spot where the deer may be vulnerable.

If you have bagged a buck, or even several, check your hunting journal to look for any key information that will help you. If you don't have a hunting journal, it's time to start one. Keeping a detailed log is a better way to accurately reconstruct the specific details of a hunt than just recalling the event from your memory. Even if the particulars of each hunting season seem totally different, and even if you did not actually bag a deer,

Mature bucks like to rub trees that are four to six inches in diameter. They rub in the direction they are traveling. A radical bowhunter should see that this is the sign of a big buck heading into his bedding area. Next step is to pick your ambush spot. JOHN DZIZA

there may be important similarities in things that did not seem significant at the time.

Look for things that relate not only to the hunting conditions, but also to the actions of the deer. If you don't have this level of information, it's a good idea to begin keeping a detailed journal this season. A radical bowhunter keeps meticulous records to gain insight into whitetail behavior, pattern individual bucks, and learn more about a specific area, especially if hunting the same area from year to year.

When reviewing journal records of successful hunts, you will probably find that although the time of day or weather was different from entry to entry, one thing was consistent in all of your experiences: Although you killed the deer, he didn't make any obvious mistakes. Usually a buck does just what he is supposed to do, following the principles of whitetail behavior. Not that he isn't flexible or adaptable, but he always does his best to remain safe, using the terrain and wind to provide him with as much security as possible. Study the lay of the land so that you can choose stand locations that will capitalize on the buck's natural inclination to keep the wind in his nose as he takes the path of least resistance.

This buck exposed himself for a few moments as he crossed this open area on his way to dense cover. It could be his weak spot and a fantastic place for a radical bowhunter to set up. JOHN DZIZA

Putting the pieces of the puzzle together by analyzing all the buck sign in an area helps me determine my ambush locations.

LOOK FOR VULNERABLE SPOTS

It's important to learn the daylight movement routes of the mature buck you are hunting because, depending on the wind and the phase of the rut, there is typically a spot along those routes that is less than ideal for concealment or safety. It is there that he will be exposed and vulnerable, even if for just a short time. Although this weak spot is less than ideal for a buck, it is a perfect spot for you to set up. A buck may have to expose himself for a few moments to get where his body is telling him to go. Finding one of these spots will take some time and work, but setting up your stand there will give you the best shooting opportunity at a buck.

Start by examining the geographic and structural characteristics of the area. Check aerial or topographical maps and look for ridges, saddles, ravines, and any other structures that will force deer movement in a particular direction. A whitetail buck is concerned first and foremost with survival; safety and security are usually uppermost in his thoughts. Understanding that, coupled with the fact that a whitetail will travel the path of least resistance, will help you locate the long-used routes that provide cover and protection while allowing a deer to sense danger coming at him by paying attention to the wind.

Knowing the exact timing of the rut and the phase you're hunting can help you determine whether the buck will be placing more emphasis on finding a hot doe or food. As the rut approaches, bucks extend their territories in search of does. During the rut, when the buck's hormones are raging, he will be distracted enough to be less cautious than normal, becoming somewhat more assailable.

Once you've found that "Achilles' heel" spot and are tuned in to the timing of the rut, you need to determine the prevailing wind patterns and specific wind directions. Make sure you use the wind to your advantage when hunting this ambush spot—you can be sure your buck will be. A whitetail's survival depends on using the wind to detect and avoid predators. The weak spot in his defense might be a location along his travel route where the wind patterns can give you an advantage or the buck may have to work without using it for a few moments. Look for places where a trail curves or bends or the deer must come across a narrow ridge or saddle.

The most important ingredient to your success is to pinpoint the deer foods that are most preferred in the area you hunt. During the early part of the bowhunting season, you should set up close to heavily used feeding areas where you have observed buck activity. If you see some bucks from your setup location, stay in that area. But if you are not seeing any buck activity, move your setup far from the feed area.

The easiest way to locate prime feeding areas is to simply drive around during the last hour of daylight and check out likely looking places. The great thing about this technique is that you can check many potential hot spots in a very short time with a spotting scope mounted on the side window of your vehicle.

OBSERVING THE DEER'S MOVEMENTS

Years ago, when I was doing deer studies with deer biologist Jimmy McDonough, I learned an important lesson. He told me that if you want to become an excellent bowhunter, you have to hunt, then stop hunting to watch and learn; only later do you hunt again. Initially you have to sacrifice, but it is a trade-off that will pay great rewards in the future. You will gain more knowledge about the deer movement patterns in your area than you would from years of sitting in your primary hunting location.

This observation process involves sitting at a location during the peak of the rut where you can observe deer movement through a corridor or natural funnel. The more of the area you can observe, the better. Your goal is to watch the deer coming and going from where you plan to hunt them. It's kind of like hunting from afar. You can even carry your bow with you, just in case, but during my experiences working with Jimmy, we never had a good buck in range for a shot. At the time, I was just a young kid who thought I knew everything and said to myself, "This guy is crazy!" But I listened and went with him, and I learned a valuable life lesson from this friend and mentor. I use what I learned every time I enter the deer woods.

Here is a case in point. Jimmy and I took up a position in a cut cornfield overlooking a few hundred yards of wood line. On the north end of the cut cornfield was a river, and on the opposite end was a sparse woods of oak and maple trees that led to thick, almost impenetrable highbush laurel. That was the bedding area. We hung a treestand in a large oak from which I could observe the field all the way to the river, as well as the fence and woodlines on both sides. In four days, during which I spent long hours glassing the terrain, I learned the routes the deer most frequently used to cross the cut cornfield. I was amazed to discover that the major route across that field was straight across the middle. I had not noticed it before because from my old setup location, I had been unable to see the deer because of the slope of the land. From this vantage point in the woodline, we documented a significant amount of buck activity and two dandy bucks. It was virtually a hotbed of rutting activity. Later we realized that they frequented this spot each year. I set up a ground blind and treestand in that area and bagged two bucks over 150 class in two years. At this point, I finally realized that Jimmy was right—as he usually is. The reason I never witnessed any of this deer activity before was I was hunting in the wrong place. I could literally write a chapter in this book on many other examples but I'll spare you because the point is made. Let the big bucks tell you where to set up your actual hunting location and you will be much more successful.

AVOIDING SPOOKING THE DEER

A radical bowhunter needs to keep a low profile and make an extremely delicate approach while on scouting missions. Many bowhunters erroneously believe that monster bucks will tolerate a human's presence. To minimize spooking deer, maintain at least 250 yards between the deer and your scouting position. Many hunters get excited when they see a monster buck and just have to get closer and closer to him. Some want to take a picture to show their friends the big buck they found and will be hunting. Take a picture of the buck after you put an arrow through him and he is on the ground, or you may not get that opportunity at all. Hunters must take every precaution possible to keep from spooking the deer. Even being detected by the immature bucks, fawns, and does in the area can send up red flags. Remain invisible while scouting if you want to be successful once you actually start to hunt.

The trophy-class bucks are highly tuned in to their home ranges during the season and can detect the slightest disturbance. So in order to be successful, you must be mobile and rotate between several different setup locations. Many hunters, thinking they have taken all the precautions necessary to ensure that their presence is totally undetectable, hunt one setup location for several days—and end up repatterning the buck. It's best to avoid hunting from the exact same setup location two days in a row. Overhunting a site can kill the location just as quickly as any other hunter error. If you do bump out a good buck, a good rule of thumb is to wait a minimum of five days for the area to settle back to normal.

CLUES DURING THE RUT

While you are sitting on stand early in the rut, listen intently for any sounds of buck activity, such as grunting, rubbing trees, or sparring. Following the sounds can help you tweak your setup location and bring you closer to the shot opportunity you have been waiting for all year. This early rut activity marks one of the prime times to kill a good buck, because they are at least somewhat patternable and are still in their bachelor groups. A radical bowhunter will take advantage here. If you are set up properly at this time of the season, it's conceivable that you could have a parade of quality bucks march by your location well within bow range.

When the rut starts to peak, forget trying to pattern a buck. Now is the time to hunt the terrain funnels that allow you to see a long way. From there, you will be able to see any buck that is chasing a doe or has been bumped out by hunting pressure. These funnels come in all shapes and sizes. Draws, strips of timber, thick brushy fencelines, and grassy ravines all can offer attractive travel corridors for bucks, and you should be looking at these features when deciding where to set up. Thick is good, but thicker is better. If a trophy buck has a chance, he will always choose an overgrown ditch or brushy strip over any other travel route. If you have seen a good buck earlier in the season moving along a creek bottom, ridge, or draw that is within a few hundred acres of a cropfield, there's an excellent chance he will use that funnel often while he is on the prowl looking for does. Higher doe concentrations in these areas will increase the odds dramatically that your buck will be cruising the area chasing or scent-checking for a doe.

When scouting a new area, walk fencelines, because they often lead to a good huntable funnel. It's also a productive way to locate deer in a new area and get a handle on the amount of deer traffic. Start at a corner or some easy access point, and as you walk the fence, look for places where the deer are crawling under or going through a hole in the fence or where the top wire is low enough for the deer to jump over easily. Look for sign such as deer hair on the fence, tracks on both sides, and well-worn deer

A monster buck made this rub; just look at the size of the tree. This is exactly the type of buck sign a radical bowhunter looks for when selecting setup locations.

Fresh scrapes like this one, found close to a bedding area, are good places to set up before the rut bursts into full bloom.
JOHN DZIZA

runs that are ninety degrees to the fence. Mark each of these places with orange surveyor's tape.

When you get to the end of the fenceline, turn around and go back the same way you came. As you walk, note the areas with the most pieces of tape grouped closely together. Check out all the areas that have multiple crossings and sign, and set up a scouting camera at each one to confirm your observations. After you have determined which are the best two crossings, set up treestands at each place within fifteen to twenty yards of the trail leading away from the fence. If there aren't any trees suitable for stands, put up ground blinds. Set up another stand or blind where you can watch the fenceline for a good distance. A radical bowhunter strategically sets up a couple more treestands or blinds so that he can rotate among the stands for hunting and watching.

CHAPTER 13

Set Up Where You Have All the Advantages

A spot is good only if you can get a shot with your bow without being seen, smelled, or heard. Whitetails have a keen detection system and will easily detect a hunter perched in a tree or sitting in a ground blind that is set up improperly and sticks out like a sore thumb.

A myriad of predators have pursued whitetails so long that the deer are adept at survival. They have learned to detect any foreign intrusion into their home territory, and that includes those on the ground as well as elevated ones. A radical bowhunter needs to set up correctly to put the odds in his favor.

Several factors are important for successful stand or blind hunting. Scouting is critical to gaining an understanding of deer movement and behavior. This will provide the key information about how and where to place a stand or blind.

Effective treestand or ground-blind hunting must include a strategy that is flexible. Whitetails develop an intricate system of travel routes within their home territory. This network enables them to avoid ambush and detection while on their way to and from their feeding and bedding grounds. They may have a dozen or more paths to the same spot, as well as escape routes that they can use to flee if they are alerted to danger. If you have set up only one stationary treestand or ground blind, your chances of being on the right trail at the right time may be slim. It's also important to set up treestands or ground blinds in several locations to avoid detection at various times and in changing conditions.

Weather influences deer movements when windy or rainy days create a backdrop of sound that they find confusing. With a buck's sense of hearing impeded by the thrashing of branches or falling rain, he sticks close to his bedding area for safety and security.

A radical bowhunter determines several locations early in the season where he will have all the advantages for success. WILDLIFE RESEARCH CENTER

Localities of activity may change after the leaves fall from the trees, as white-tailed deer seek areas that afford cover. They search for dense pines, tall brush, thick stands of trees, any place that will help camouflage their presence. Places that had dense growth in the spring and summer may be abandoned for more secure locations in the fall during the hunting season, especially as the season progresses, because there will be less and less cover. Don't set up your stand or ground blind in an area that looks great in August but will be barren in October.

When looking for quality stand or blind locations, consider the following:

- Hone in on any low spots and very narrow crossings of creeks and fencerows. These natural funnels are prime locations to set up for big bucks.
- Look for ridge saddles, shallow ditches, and other subtle contours of the land that will direct deer movement past a setup location.
- If you hunt an area with field crops such as alfalfa, corn, or soybeans, investigate the harvest time. When the crops are harvested, the deer patterns will change in the entire area.
- Deer will travel the edges where stands of dark timber such as heavy pines and hardwoods meet all year long.

Let your scouting camera point you to the right location to erect a treestand or ground blind. WILDLIFE RESEARCH CENTER

- Deer will move between cropfields and timber along heavily brushed and tree-lined fencerows.
- Mature bucks like to bed in thickets on ridges or hillsides.
- Mature bucks will browse and bed in and around power lines and clear-cuts, especially if they are off the beaten path.
- Be aware of hunter movements. You don't want to place a setup near areas where hunters will be passing through and disturbing deer or, worse yet, blowing your setup.

Paramount to finding the right locations to place your treestands or ground blinds is good scouting, ideally before the hunting season begins. Scouting is essential so that you can pinpoint areas where deer activity is high. It will also enable you to pattern the deer in the area so that you will have several prime sites to place your setup, be it a treestand or ground blind. Remember mobility is vital.

Prepare and set up your ambush sites early. This will enable you to create clear shooting lanes by snipping branches or chopping limbs to increase your effectiveness. Be especially careful not to remove too much cover while you are creating your shooting lanes. Often bowhunters clear out their hunting spots so well that they repattern the mature bucks right

A tree like this with monster rubs, in an area close to dense cover, is an optimal location for a treestand or ground blind. JOHN DZIZA

out of the area for the balance of the hunting season. Starting early will also give the deer time to settle down after your intrusion.

A quality treestand or ground blind can offer one of the greatest advantages you can have in your pursuit of a trophy buck, so select your equipment with care. Many manufacturers offer light, strong, compact treestands with a minimum of moving parts. I like Rivers Edge Treestands line of quality climbers and hang-on stands and Double Bull Archery ground blinds. Quality treestands and blinds are easy to set up and mount, and most important, they are quiet. One clink of metal during the hunting season and your setup site will be useless. Your treestand or ground blind also should allow you to move to a new location easily so that if you are detected or the deer retreat to a different area, you will not waste your entire season sitting in a cold spot with no deer.

Being flexible and mobile are essential to a radical bowhunter's success. If a stand is not productive, don't try to wait it out; rarely will it get better. Carefully and quietly move to a new location. Stationary treestands or ground blinds make this impossible, and this type of hunting just won't remain effective after a day or two, if that long. Make your hunting sites as flexible and responsive to change as the big bucks you are bowhunting and watch your overall success increase.

REMAINING UNDETECTED

If whitetails detect human odor, they often wait to confirm the presence via another sense. Sometimes they will pass under a treestand and not be alarmed even though they may sense your presence. This may be because they have been conditioned to hunter presence, but if you are still and quiet, they simply may not see you as a threat. Rest assured, however, that they will be wary. Other times they will send out a chemical warning to other deer by stamping their feet, which deposits a scent on the ground that will remain to alert other whitetails for many days.

A radical bowhunter will always be critically aware of eliminating his human scent by using Scent Killer liquid soap, shampoo, and anti-perspirant and deodorant until he is squeaky clean and scent-free. I would never think of hunting without wearing a fully activated Scent-Lok suit with head cover and gloves combined with their BaseSlayers undergarments to insure total scent protection. I had hunted for many years without the protection these products afford, and now I say to all radical bowhunters: You cannot afford to enter the deer woods without this type of protection. The technology is there. It levels the playing field. Do the math, as they say, and use it!

Deer may also detect you by sight. Not only are they able to detect the slightest change in their environment, but they can see colors as well.

If you want to get within the killing zone, make sure the buck you are pursuing cannot smell you. WILDLIFE RESEARCH CENTER

Human skin color is discernible in the woods, so camouflage your face and hands by wearing a full head cover and gloves. Use camouflage patterns that blend with the natural surrounding as closely as possible. If you are using a treestand, it's a good idea to cover the floor and lower half of your stand area with a camouflage material so that when you are sitting, all that is visible from the ground is your upper body from the shoulders up. This screen also will hide a lot of your movement, muffle sound, and block the wind from your body.

White-tailed deer naturally move during the low-light times of day—dawn and dusk—as well as the night. Their eyes are designed for catching all available light, so unlike humans, they can see ultraviolet light. Many fabrics today are treated with brighteners that reflect this ultraviolet light, and detergents add brighteners to each wash. So while you sit perched silently in your stand, your clothing may be a screaming beacon to the deer, flashing your presence to them. Many quality outdoor clothing manufacturers do not use brighteners in their products, and some products eliminate the ultraviolet problem, such as Wildlife Research Products' Clothing Wash or Carbo Wash or Scent-Lok's premium clothing wash.

Despite all these precautions, within twenty-four to forty-eight hours of being occupied for any length of time, most treestands will have been identified and the deer will have begun avoiding them. And for bowhunters who do not follow careful techniques to minimize noise, scent, and visibility, their treestand or ground-blind locations may be ruined almost immediately, the first time they are used. White-tailed deer, especially mature bucks, will move out and circle the area about one hundred yards away—safe, out of range, but close enough to know what is going on. So despite your best efforts at avoiding detection, this keen whitetail security system makes it imperative that you have alternate sites available.

CHAPTER 14

Choose the Smartest— Not Shortest— Way to Your Stand

A radical bowhunter never takes the easy route if it means possibly alerting a big buck to his presence. A weekend bowhunter looks for an easy place to park his vehicle, takes a short walk to his hunting spot, then complains to everyone about seeing only a few does, very small bucks, or nothing at all. Unfortunately many bowhunters blow their cover long before they ever reach their hunting locations. Much of your success depends on how and when you enter and leave your stand or blind.

You need to understand the general travel routes of the white-tailed deer you plan to hunt in order to get to your hunting location without disturbing any of them. Many things have to be taken into consideration when moving to and from your hunting spot. If it is a morning approach, are the deer still going to be feeding along the route you will be strolling? Will your afternoon route take you on a hike right through the prime bedding area of the buck you are hunting? It is a good idea to plan out these routes well before the season. Take time to prepare and cut silent approaches through heavy cover and scrape or rake leaves away from your walking path. Lay a fallen log or two in any trouble spots where you think noise may make a difference, so that you can walk on the log to get across the area more quietly.

Most guys in the deer woods never think of the importance of getting from point A to point B and back again. They are so anxious to get into and out of their hunting spots that they never consider the consequences. Many bowhunters have learned they need to travel to their stand locations for evening hunts while the deer are bedded down. It is equally important to have the patience to stay at your stand location until the deer have completely departed the area. It will take a very short time for

Every radical bowhunter's worst fear: a whitetail fleeing the area after discerning the hunter's arrival. JOHN DZIZA

Marching across these fields to your ambush site will most assuredly result in your not seeing anything to ambush. Easiest access is never the best route for a radical bowhunter. JOHN DZIZA

the white-tailed deer to pattern you if they hear you getting out and leaving your ambush spot. Every mature buck I have encountered over the years had this uncanny ability for locating bowhunters on stand and then detouring well around the area, safely out of the range of their bows. Having pinpointed the location of a hunter, they continue to avoid him and his stand area, not for just a day, but for the remainder of the hunting season and maybe even longer.

Several years ago, I was bowhunting a small woodlot in northern Missouri, using a deep creek bottom for the route to my hunting location. I had just settled in when I noticed the landowner of the property arrive and watched him approach his stand. He parked his pickup truck, then marched toward the woodlot half a mile across the harvested soybean and cornfields. I asked myself, "What is this guy doing? Does he think he is invisible or something?" Then I watched more than a dozen deer, which included at least three bucks over 140-class, bolt out the back door of the woodlot. He sat all day hunting those guys, but they were long gone.

If the deer are feeding while you are approaching your hunting location and you spook them, you just blew your opportunity to hunt them today, tomorrow, and maybe even the next day. It's critical that you take the time and effort to circle any such areas on the way to your spot so you won't blow the deer out of that area. A radical bowhunter always wants the wind to flow from the deer toward the hunter, so they will not detect human scent.

Not only is it critical to keep your hunting location advantageous with respect to the direction of the wind, but you also must keep your travel routes to your hunting spot free from human scent. If you haven't taken the proper precautions before entering the woods, every step you take is leaving a scent trail that could spook or totally repattern the deer you are about to hunt. Always wear rubber boots when going to and from your deer-hunting stand to minimize the transfer of odors from your feet to the ground and its cover. Take all the other precautions necessary to become as scent-free as possible before traveling to your hunting location. Do not let any exposed skin touch any foliage on the way in or out of your hunting location, because your scent will remain up to several days.

Often, the walk to your hunting location will require some effort. In these situations, a radical bowhunter will dress for the occasion by traveling light to minimize any perspiration. Wear a Scent-Lok backpack with the heavier Scent-Lok Dakota insulated parka or a windproof fleece outfit and any other gear needed, including a Scent-Lok head cover packed inside. A radical bowhunter is meticulous and fanatical about scent control, because we stink to a white-tailed deer. Imagine that you are a skunk that just walked into a beauty parlor. What do you think the women's reaction would be to you? Now multiply that odor by a factor of ten.

While you are moving, vary your steps. Change the length of each stride and the interval between rests, and sometimes walk in a quick burst. White-tailed deer have adapted over the years to be able to easily identify hunters by our even and monotonous stride. They will think you are something else and not be alarmed if they hear variations in your footsteps. As unbelievable as it sounds, I have even had deer come over to me to investigate the source of the movement. They got within a few yards of me, pushing their noses in my direction to try to wind what I was and pointing and pivoting their ears to try to pick up a sound, as I stood motionless not making eye contact.

On very windy days, try walking only when the wind is gusting hard and listening and watching for deer when the gust stops. Several years ago, I watched a mature buck actually crouch down and try to sneak low past me. Another behavior a deer may use is to just lie there with its head on the ground and let you walk right past. Once you have gone, the deer will slip right out the back door. These animals are fighting for their

A GPS system will help any radical bowhunter preplot entry and exit routes to stand or ground-blind locations.
JOHN DZIZA

survival and will do whatever it takes to avoid any predator, and we are the ultimate predator. It is impossible for even a radical bowhunter to know where the deer are all the time, but focusing on details will pay rewarding dividends in the end.

When you need to walk under the cover of darkness, use a green-tinted flashlight for entry and exit to your hunting location. It will illuminate nearly as well as a white bulb for the human eye, and you can shine the green light right into a deer's eyes without bothering them. When you shut it off, it does not affect your night vision, so your eyes will not have to readjust.

Another valuable hunting aid that will enable you to plot your entry and exit routes perfectly so you will have no trouble getting into your spot is a quality GPS unit. A radical bowhunter takes advantage of GPS technology, not only for pinpoint accuracy when scouting, but also for preplotting an unobtrusive way to the stand.

Excitement and anticipation can make you a foolish bowhunter. Take your time to think things through and listen to your surroundings before making any movement in the deer woods. A radical bowhunter always sets out a plan with a goal at the end. That goal is to succeed.

Here, I check my GPS unit as I safely enter the deer woods on the way to my treestand. JOHN DZIZA

This huge-bodied, heavy-racked buck from southern Saskatchewan is what the radical bowhunter dreams of season after season. JOHN DZIZA

I harvested this monster buck in southern Iowa, on a prime piece of property managed for trophy whitetails.

A radical bowhunter is not bound by traditional means. Using a mountain bike to get deep into the woods will get you where the deer have gone to avoid the pressure from other hunters. You can bike in quickly, easily, and quietly to hunt areas others think are too far or too difficult.

An established food plot will attract deer like a magnet.

Right before the season begins, place a scouting camera just off a well-used feed area and hang a curiosity lure from a scent wick to get photos of the bucks frequenting the area and find possible ambush sites.

WILDLIFE RESEARCH CENTER

Look closely; can you see the radical bowhunter in this photo? Using the right camo can make a hunter virtually invisible. Match your background.

A ground blind can be an excellent option for long-day hunts, providing you with some freedom of movement without being spotted by deer.

JOHN DZIZA

*The radical bowhunter always ensures
that his bow is absolutely silent
during the draw and release.*

JOHN DZIZA

*Watch and listen intently for thirty
minutes after your rattling sequence.
This is one time when too much is
not too good. Be patient.*

JOHN DZIZA

An effective spot to try rattling a buck in is outside his bedroom.

JOHN DZIZA

A rare shot of a buck returning a vocalization on his approach, which is unusual. Always be alert when calling. A buck is able to pinpoint your exact location.

JOHN DZIZA

Here, I'm dragging out the 160-class buck I harvested from a treestand while hunting a swamp.

JOHN DZIZA

Author Dick Scorzafava, the radical bowhunter.

JOHN DZIZA

When all else fails, blindside them! JOHN DZIZA

In the right situation, using a ground blind fashioned out of natural materials can be radical.

JOHN DZIZA

PART FOUR

HOW:

Bring big bucks close to you

CHAPTER 15

Coaxing Bucks with Decoys

If you don't use a decoy, you're missing out on one of the top tools for bagging big bucks. A decoy is a must-have for every radical bowhunter. Using decoys gives you a glimpse of deer behavior not usually witnessed by the majority of hunters, letting you see how white-tailed bucks react to another deer. Observing these relationships between deer provides you with valuable insight, and this is a fascinating and exciting way to watch one of nature's unbelievable dramas unfold before your eyes.

Decoys can be instrumental in improving success during deer-hunting season, but two elements—proper setup and timing—must be understood in order to use these hunting aids effectively. To help you better understand these factors, along with my own tips and techniques, this chapter presents some decoy know-how from three well-known and respected North American whitetail hunters. The experts whose words of wisdom we will share here are Ian McMurchy from Saskatchewan, Canada; Gary Clancy from Minnesota; Charlie Alsheimer from New York. These men have more experience using decoys for white-tailed deer hunting than anyone on the planet. Let's see what they have to say.

IAN MCMURCHY

Ian McMurchy has been using decoys for almost twenty years and was one of the pioneers who boldly began using the first decoys. Working near his home in Saskatchewan, Canada, he took most of the original photographs that were published by various decoy manufacturers. Not only does he use decoys nearly every day he hunts, but he always uses them when he is photographing white-tailed deer in the wild. He has achieved great results in both endeavors.

Adding an attractant lure
to the tail of your doe
decoy will use two of the
buck's senses: sight and
smell. JOHN DZIZA

McMurchy recognizes that the timing of decoy use is critical. He recommends using a doe decoy anytime during the season, reminding
hunters that deer will generally come across a field to feed with another
deer. Conversely, he makes limited use of buck decoys, employing them
only during prerut and rut periods, which run roughly from October 15
through November 30, when bucks are exhibiting dominance and territorial behaviors.

During the early season, using a doe decoy, McMurchy cuts an apple
in half and rubs it all over the nose and mouth areas. His reasoning is that
deer are controlled by their stomachs. They always smell each other along
the snout and mouth to find out what the other has been eating. He has
actually had deer come right up and lick the apple juice off the decoy.

During the prerut and rut phases, McMurchy follows a different scent
strategy. For doe decoys, he applies an attractant lure to the rump and
down the back legs. Buck decoys require a bit of a different tactic, using a
dominant buck lure on the back legs and forehead.

Placement of decoys is critical and should look realistic. Put the buck decoy behind the doe so other bucks think he is following the doe. JOHN DZIZA

When using a Tail-Wagger, set it up with the wagging tail facing the opposite direction of the other decoys in the group. Incoming deer will see the tail moving back and forth, and the body language will speak to them. JOHN DZIZA

Don't be afraid to be creative when using decoys. For example, you can remove a decoy's legs and lay it down to resemble a bedded deer. This can help relax any other deer passing through the area and boost their confidence.

McMurchy says that whitetails are creatures of edge effect. Set up your decoy on an edge where a trail comes into a field or clearing. Make it look as if it is entering from the trail rather than exiting.

Multiple decoys can also provide good success. McMurchy likes to set up a doe and a buck together, as if the buck were tending the doe. He says this is his most effective decoy ploy.

McMurchy also believes that it helps to provide some implied motion to your decoy, bringing them to life. He uses a Tail-Wagger by Come-Alive Decoy Company. It's so effective that he even has turkeys come right into the area and feed next to his decoy.

GARY CLANCY

Minnesotan Gary Clancy is the author of the book *Rattling, Calling, and Decoying Whitetails*, based on more than a decade of experimenting with decoys. Clancy says his best results come from using decoys between October 20 and November 20, year in and year out. He has not found much success with decoys early or late in the season, so he does what works for him, employing them with great, consistent results during that short window of time.

Clancy is another big believer in providing motion to a decoy, and he uses an electric Tail-Wagger where they are legal. Where they are not legal, he creates his own movement by using one-by-four-inch strips cut from a white plastic trash bag, which is stirred by even the slightest breeze. He recommends using a strip on each ear and one on the rump. He attaches them by heating a small nail with a lighter, then pushing it through a plastic strip and into the decoy.

Contaminating your decoy with human scent is a critical error, and Clancy cautions hunters to always wear rubber gloves when handling a decoy. For that magic touch of scent, he uses an attractant lure such as Wildlife Research Center's Excite or Special Golden Estrus doe-in-estrus scent on a doe decoy, and their Mega-Tarsal Plus lure or even fresh tarsal glands on buck decoys. He does not apply the scent directly to the decoy, but prefers to use a footlong stick with a Pro Scent Wick attached to one end. He saturates the wick with lure and sticks the other end into the ground between the decoy's legs.

Clancy uses full-body decoys most of the time, but he has also had good results with the less expensive and easier-to-carry silhouettes. He has the best results when using a decoy in conjunction with calling and rattling, and he believes that the decoy just provides a little insurance to the buck that there is really a deer there. A decoy adds a visual image to those sound effects.

CHARLIE ALSHEIMER

Charlie Alsheimer lives in upstate New York and is field editor for *Deer and Deer Hunting* magazine. He has authored several books on deer hunting and has been using decoys for more than a decade. Alsheimer finds that using decoys in areas where baiting is legal does not work well. He says his best results come from using decoys ten to fourteen days before the peak of the does' breeding cycle.

Alsheimer recommends carrying the decoy unassembled in a bag when traveling in the woods. This hides it from other hunters who may catch a glimpse of it and mistakenly think you are a deer moving through the woods. When you get about seventy-five to a hundred yards from where you plan to hunt, stop and assemble the decoy, place some blaze orange on it, and then carry it to your hunting spot. Take care in anchoring the decoy to the ground and eliminating or removing all human scent. Alsheimer sprays the entire decoy with Scent Killer and then leaves it alone.

Set up your decoys in an area where they can be seen from a distance. JOHN DZIZA

He says it's important to set your decoy in a place where it can be seen, such as in an open hardwood spot or at the edge of a field. If you are using a buck decoy, he says you'll have better results if you place the decoy facing you. Bucks, he finds, will usually approach a buck decoy from the side or front, very seldom from behind. If you are using a doe decoy, setup is just the opposite, because bucks usually approach a doe from behind. A doe decoy should be facing away from you, so that you are looking at the rump. Set up the decoy about twenty-five yards from your stand.

Alsheimer also believes that decoys need motion. He has experienced more than 50 percent rejection when using a decoy without any action. His secret is to attach a white handkerchief to the rump of the decoy. He then ties 10-pound-test monofilament fishing line to the end of the handkerchief and runs the line to his stand. He secures the line to his boot and moves his foot to move the handkerchief on the decoy. It's simple and effective, and it keeps his hands free for using his bow.

When a buck approaches a decoy, decide whether you want to take him before he gets to the decoy. Alsheimer warns that when the buck gets there, he will be thrashing around the decoy, and it might be difficult to get a shot off.

Finally, he warns never to leave your decoy out in the area you are hunting when you are not actively hunting. Once a buck interacts with a decoy, he will learn to avoid them.

DECOYS FOR THE RADICAL BOWHUNTER

My own experiences hunting with decoys have been favorable. I have had very good results decoying bucks about two weeks before the peak of the rut. For some reason, I have not had positive results with decoys at other times, so I tend to focus on using them when they work the best for me. Doe decoys seem to bring me better results than buck decoys. Setting up a doe and buck combination, with the buck directly behind the doe, has also worked very well.

It is critical that your decoy be scent-free. I wash my decoy down with Scent Killer odor-eliminating soap and store it in a Scent-Lok storage bag until I use it. I never handle it without rubber gloves. After setting it up, I give it a spray of a Scent Killer odor-eliminating product. I have found that not only is it important to anchor your decoy, but it is crucial to make sure that the decoy appears to be standing naturally. If it is leaning at all, it will look out of kilter to the deer, and they will avoid it.

Motion is essential for the decoy to be effective; without it, a decoy looks like a statue. I too have had excellent results with a tailwagger, where I could legally use one. When I can't use one, I improvise with white chicken feathers. I tie two or three onto a fine thread or fishing line and tape them to the butt of the decoy. I also attach a single feather on a short bit of thread in front of each ear. That way I get movement in the front as well as the rear of my decoy.

I add some lure to the rump and rear legs of the decoy. Special Golden Estrus doe-in-estrus scent is my favorite. It works for me because of the time in the breeding cycle that I use a decoy. Vocalizations from a buck grunt gives further realism to the decoy. When you incorporate a grunt call, you are using all three of a buck's key senses to pull him in to your decoy: sight, scent, and hearing.

Decoys are a great aid to add to your bag of deer-hunting tricks, and every radical bowhunter will surely want to try using this approach. Keep your personal safety the number-one objective in any hunting plan. Decoys can be a fun way to increase the excitement of your white-tailed deer bowhunting experience, but they can confuse hunters the same way they confuse deer. Before you set up decoys, find out whether anyone else is hunting the area. If so, let them know you are using a decoy setup.

Using multiple decoys adds to the realism. JOHN DZIZA

TIPS FOR USING A DECOY

- For your safety, carry your unassembled decoy into your hunting area in a blaze orange bag.
- Wear rubber gloves when handling a decoy, and after it has been set up, spray it with Scent-Killer spray.
- Set up your decoy within your shooting range, in a clear shooting lane.
- Set up your decoy in a high-use area on a trail with buck sign. Place it in the open so it is easily visible, yet close to nearby thick cover.
- Use bedded decoys only in multiple setups. Never place them on a trail. They work best on the edges of cropfields.
- Place your decoy upwind from where you expect deer to enter.
- A doe decoy should have the butt facing your setup location. Bucks will approach the decoy from the side or rear.
- A buck decoy should have the head facing your setup location. Bucks will come in straight-on to try to intimidate another buck.
  - Add realism to your setup with attractant lures and movement. You can also incorporate calling and rattling to take advantage of the buck's sense of hearing.

CHAPTER 16

Rattling His Cage

When bucks fight, all deer listen . . . and come running. Knowing how and when to rattle in the biggest bucks in the woods is a tactic that all radical bowhunters need in their bag of tricks. Rattling is an essential technique for every bowhunter who wants to bag a monster buck. When combined with proper calling, a decoy, and attractant lures, it can bring an elusive buck into a bowhunter's range for a good, clean shot. This is especially true in dense areas where you need to get the deer in extremely close to be able to see him before you can even take a shot.

If banging together a couple of old bones works in one spot, shouldn't it work in another? Well, first of all, there is more to rattling than just banging a couple of antlers together. There is a specific pattern to the technique that must be followed, or else the sounds you create will be out of sequence and foreign—you might just as well whistle for a whitetail buck.

For rattling, a radical bowhunter uses natural whitetail antlers, either sheds or antlers cut off a skull plate. Real antlers are superior to manufactured plastic antlers or rattling bags. The other products just do not sound like the natural antlers; they will not give the higher notes you want to hear when you really smash them together. If you use sheds, they must be good, green, fresh ones. Avoid white, bleached-out, or cracked antlers, because they have lost their natural ring at this point. A medium set is a great size to use because they are the most versatile, and you can make them sound like just about any size buck with a little practice. I prefer 130-class antlers with a wide, sweeping beam rather than one with a tight rack. A wide beam will save your fingers and knuckles, especially if you remove the brow tines. Drill a hole through each antler at the base of the main beam, and thread a long boot lace through the hole for carrying them in and out of the woods.

Here again, safety is a concern. The noise made by someone smashing antlers together to sound like a couple bucks engaged in a street fight gets a lot of people really excited and pumped up. If you can fool the deer, you can fool another hunter. Make sure everyone in your hunting party knows you will be rattling and from where. Do not rattle in the midst of any other hunters who are unaware of your presence, because it is extremely dangerous. Making your presence known beforehand could save your life.

Every season, we hear stories about a monster buck that came charging in to a hunter who was crashing antlers together very loudly to simulate two bucks really going at each other. The bowhunter wasn't ready with his bow and missed his golden opportunity at the buck of his dreams.

Many bowhunters believe rattling is effective only during the rut and about a week before and a week after. In reality, however, bucks spar with each other from the time they shed the velvet from their antlers until well after the rut has ended. A whitetail buck will spar for several reasons. Young bucks spar in play and to determine their place in the pecking order. Most times the older mature bucks spar to test each other, although these matches never develop into full-blown street fights until the rut. This is dependent on the buck-to-doe ratio in the area you are hunting. The closer to even it is, the more competition there will be for the does, and consequently the more intense the buck fights will be in that area.

The really serious street fights usually happen between two bucks that are equally matched and have not crossed paths with each other. They never had the opportunity to work out their dominance in the pecking order. These situations occur when a buck is cruising between doe family units out of his home range during the peak of the rut. Deer are curious creatures, and just like humans going to see a house on fire, just to see what happened, other bucks come to the fight to see who will be the winner of the battle.

Many of us hunt in heavily populated areas mainly because we live nearby. This ease of access and the fact that we are probably very familiar with these hunting grounds make them reasonable places to hunt. Another factor is that when a hunter has success in an area, he usually feels good about returning there—and so perhaps do a bunch of other hunters, especially if he has shared his exploits and his hunting location with his buddies. Word travels fast.

The key to rattling in these heavily populated and pressured areas is in the actual setup—specifically, where you set up and how. For years, I didn't have much success rattling here in the Northeast unless I was in

Rattling in thick cover can be a productive tactic for attracting bucks anywhere that you hunt whitetails. JOHN DZIZA

the less pressured big woods of Maine, New Hampshire, or Vermont. I mistakenly used the same strategy as in places like Iowa, Illinois, Montana, or Saskatchewan, areas that offer some great hunting on a large expanse of acreage that is for the most part open and virtually pressure free. It took me a while to realize that I was wrong to set up close to home the same way I did in these other places, where I had experienced much more favorable results rattling in bucks.

The problem here in the populated East is that the deer react differently to all the hunting pressure. In the less pressured areas, the bucks would aggressively approach the rattling antlers, rushing in to investigate the sounds they heard. The pressured eastern whitetails would also be attracted to the rattle, but they would cautiously circle downwind and look for the deer that were fighting. They carefully assess the airborne odors, most times staying out of range. These deer have been conditioned to be cautious because of the amounts of hunting pressure they receive.

Even in these pressured areas, I was setting up in somewhat open places where I could see—because that's the way I'd done it in most of the midwestern and western areas. Finally the light went on, and I realized that these eastern deer were under much more hunting pressure, which might be causing them to react differently to the rattling antlers. To compensate for the difference in the hunting pressure, I began setting up in the thickest cover I could find in the buck's bedroom. This ensured that he would have to advance pretty close to where the antlers were clashing together before he could see what was going on.

If you are going to rattle in pressured habitat, set up in a thick spot of hemlocks or evergreens that completely surrounds you. Make sure you have some shooting lanes that are free and clear. Choose a position that has an opening with a good downwind view. This will almost force the buck to cross your path as he circles downwind of your position. Dense cover means that you may catch only a glimpse of a rack, a white throat patch, or a leg, so pay particular attention to the cover, looking for deer parts on both sides of the opening.

To enhance the technique and to give the buck confidence as he approaches, set up several buck urine scent wicks around your stand or use an atomizer to spray the trees and foliage. You can also throw a decoy and doe calling into the mix. Place your decoy in one of the openings so the buck will be able to see it on his approach. Also add a little doe-in-estrus attractant lure to the decoy's butt area by using a white sterile cloth and tape. When you are doing this, it will use all of the buck's senses and increase your odds. I have proven to myself many times over that this is the best rattling setup to use anywhere there are white-tailed deer. I've

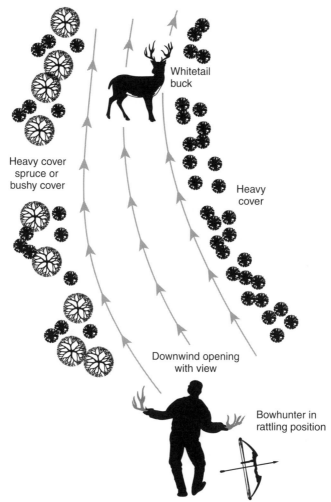

Always choose a position for rattling with a downwind view. This will force the buck to expose himself as he circles your position. A radical bowhunter will make sure he is ready to take the shot and bag the buck.

also determined that it's more productive in the morning than any other time of the day, because the buck has been up most of the night cruising around his home range, and on the way back to his bedding area, his senses are not as keen because he is tired.

These changes in technique—setting up in cover and adding a scent element—have made a world of difference in the effectiveness of rattling where I know the bucks have been exposed to high hunting pressure or in populated areas where there are thick pockets of cover. It has also

The key to rattling is where you set up.

improved my results when rattling in places with virtually no hunting pressure. These two slight variations are enough to improve the odds in any situation.

Most bowhunters realize that rattling antlers can be a useful technique, but some are still skeptical. Perhaps because they are a bit unsure of exactly where, when, or how to rattle, they use the technique only as a last-ditch effort when nothing else has worked. Popping out your rattling antlers and giving a rattle just before you leave the woods for the day will not reinforce positive feelings for this technique. Rattling once, waiting a few minutes, and then leaving for the day will be ineffective. It just doesn't work that way.

On the contrary, rattling should be carefully planned. Plan to use the technique consistently throughout an entire day. Starting at daylight, begin by producing a low-key rattling sequence, and then wait fifteen or twenty minutes. The next sequence should be more aggressive and vigorous, and add a few low grunts to imitate bucks fighting. After the first few sequences without results, make the woods ring and echo with the sound of antlers. If you are in an area where you know there are no monster bucks, however, tone down the antlers so you won't intimidate the lesser bucks in the area. Extreme rattling can spook skittish bucks right out of the area. If you are in doubt, use a lower-volume rattling sequence.

For best results, plan to use your rattling technique throughout an entire day.

If you have more than one stand location or hot spot picked out, try each location for at least two hours. Rattle, then look intently with your binoculars, listen, wait, rattle, and wait again.

It does no good to rattle where there are no rutting bucks. Sure, the blind-luck principle may pull in an odd buck, but for consistent success, you need to be very particular about where you rattle. Rattle where you find fresh buck sign. A buck that is getting ready to rut or is in the rutting phase is in an aggressive mood. This is the buck that will investigate the noise you are making to simulate another buck in his territory. The rutting buck is ready for combat. You must try to imitate the sounds that a buck would hear at that time in the woods. Not only should your rattling technique include other sounds of battle, but it also must be done at the right time and in relation to the natural sounds found in the woods.

Prerut behavior includes a lot of rubbing, not rattling. A prerut buck is less aggressive, more careful and curious. Rubbing also has its own sound sequence that will carry through the woods and bring bucks in for a closer look: a hard smack of a single antler against the trunk of a tree, accompanied by a grunt that indicates force or exertion, followed by the antler rubbing up and down the tree.

Rattling, on the other hand, begins with the sounds of stomping feet, imitated by the hunter by striking the ground with the base of the rattling antler. In trying to re-create the sounds of an actual confrontation, don't hesitate to make noise. This is an auditory technique. Make a loud snort-wheeze and crash the antlers together with much force and noise. Break branches, stomp around, and make grunt or exertion sounds. In short, match what you're doing to what the bucks would actually be doing at this time in the woods. Then stop and wait thirty or forty minutes to see if a buck is curious or furious enough to investigate the contest.

Although many bucks will race in, ready to defend their home turf, others will pick their way through the dense cover in order to get a sneak peek at whatever is making all the commotion. This may take some time, and rattling too often or not waiting long enough between sequences is not natural. The deer are used to the sounds of the forest, and if you want this technique to work, you must imitate the bucks' natural behavior as closely as possible, from stomping and clashing to grunting and crashing. It's critical to wait for those thirty or so minutes after each sequence to see if you've caught a deer's ear.

My past experiences have taught me that I have the best results hunting in a buck's bedroom in the morning. I guess I felt that because he was on the prowl all night, he'd be wearily searching for his bed with his senses lessened by fatigue. It's just like how we feel at the end of a long

For rattling to be productive, it is critical that the bowhunter maintain absolute quiet and stillness while waiting for a buck to appear after the rattling sequence. The deer may detect the slightest motion or sound and bolt to safety.
JOHN DZIZA

hard day. We are tired and may not be functioning on all eight cylinders. Anyone who has ever worked third shift knows what I mean; the sun may be shining, but if you've just come off the graveyard shift, you are like a zombie, and all you want is to get home, pull the shades, and sleep.

If possible, try to get the buck to come to you uphill. Rattle near fresh sign, and if possible, try to get uphill from the travel lanes. This will allow you to look down on the surrounding terrain and likely give you a better view from a longer distance.

Hunting in highly pressured or densely populated areas can be challenging, but it can be a rewarding experience. Not all hunters are able to strike out for wilderness areas, as they are bound by time or financial constraints. Still others want to hunt at every opportunity, and those opportunities near home seem more readily available. A radical bowhunter takes advantage of both scenarios. How then to compensate for those pressured bucks and populated locations? Rattling will give you the edge you need to draw these elusive bucks in close enough to present you with a shooting opportunity. Just remember to re-create the sounds that would be happening in the forest, and set up in a thick area where you have seen buck sign.

TIPS FOR ANTLER RATTLING

- Medium to large antlers are best for rattling, because the sound will carry much farther in the woods.
- Rattling works best at the peak of the rut, but it will work during the entire rutting period.
- Rattling works best in the morning, especially next to a prime bedding area.
- How effective rattling will be in an area is determined by the buck-to-doe ratio and the age structure of the herd, which has to have a good number of mature deer.
- A buck comes in to rattling antlers because of curiosity and desire to establish dominance in the pecking order.
- Bucks will generally approach rattling antlers from downwind.
- Add scent lures and a decoy to rattling to engage all of the buck's senses.

CHAPTER 17

Calling Big Bucks

It used to be we'd just sit in a stand location and wait for the deer to come. A radical bowhunter is proactive, however, using calls to reel in those big bucks. This brings to mind a hunt where calling helped me bag Mr. Big:

> I made a few short, snappy putt grunts on my Herdmaster deer call. Suddenly there he was to my left, slowly and deliberately heading in my direction along the river bottom. I tried to calm myself as he approached closer and closer. I was confident that I'd taken every precaution to make sure he couldn't wind me. I took a deep breath, drew my bow, picked a spot, and launched my arrow. It was a perfect hit as I watched the vanes on my arrow disappear through his rib cage. He bolted about twenty yards and piled up into a big heap right in front of me. What an incredible buck—he had thirteen heavy points and a body to match.

This was the buck I'd been hunting all season, but after many days of hunting, I finally emerged the victor. I had fooled this big buck into thinking another buck was in his area tracking a hot doe. This was two days after Thanksgiving, well after the peak of the rut here in southern Iowa. At this time of the season, the bucks are having a difficult time finding a doe that is still in heat. That is why I chose that sequence of calling, hoping it would get the old boy excited enough to come over to my stand location.

There is a full range of deer vocalizations that can match a buck's mood. It's always best to keep it simple, however, and get back to basics. My good friends Greg Hood of Southern Game Calls and Preston Pittman

This heavy-racked thirteen-point buck responded to my short, snappy putt grunts.

of Pittman Game Calls have spent many years designing and developing quality calls. Their calls are the best all-around deer calls available. They are extremely user-friendly, and the design of the megaphone barrel makes them unique. They do not have a straight bore, which allows the reed to collapse from the rear to the mouthpiece; this design keeps a truer tone and will never freeze up. The adjustable band allows you the exact articulation and level of passion that you want to put into your vocalizing.

To be successful at calling white-tailed deer, many specific fine points need to come together. There are factors you must understand about the area you plan to hunt so you can formulate a calling presentation. The following are the key ingredients to formulating a plan: the age structure of the deer herd you will be hunting; the buck-to-doe ratio in that herd; the prevailing wind direction as it relates to the deer-movement patterns;

where mature bucks spend most of their time during the time you plan to hunt the area (this can change as the season progresses, so you need to stay on top of this); and the location of all your treestand or ground-blind setups. Furthermore, it is important to understand that any whitetail buck three and a half years or older tends to behave like a solitary animal; it will react differently to calling than any other deer in the area. Once you understand how these mature animals react with regard to these factors, your odds for calling success will greatly increase.

Now you need to formulate a calling sequence. Most hunters blow a deer call like a duck call—too frequently and without enough thought about what they are actually communicating to the deer. It's not what you say, but how you say it that counts in calling any game animal; it is all in the presentation. Deer are motivated by passion and survival. If you are in a bad mood or are angry when you speak to your dog, he will be intimidated, tucking his tail between his legs and even hanging his head. Deer react in much the same manner if you are aggressive with your calling. You need to understand what type of calling will motivate the buck you are hunting for each particular day.

During opening weekend of the white-tailed deer season in Mississippi one year, Greg knew there was a large, mature buck in the public area he was planning to hunt. He also knew that on opening day, the mature whitetail buck would be very attentive to the sounds in the woods because of the heavy pressure from hunters in the area. Greg thought that because of the pressure, the buck would react to his calling presentation only if it were to match the buck's mood, so he decided to use a short yearling distress call to get his attention. He then waited five minutes before doing any more calling. He knew that all of the buck's attention would be on the area where he had heard the distress call, and he would be reluctant to move until he knew what was going on in that area. Greg followed this up with a soft, contented doe bleat to calm the buck back down, and then waited ten more minutes. Next, he used three soft rut grunts to arouse a full range of emotions in the buck. This gave the buck the illusion that he was in much better surroundings than he actually was. Within seconds, the buck returned Greg's vocalization with a soft, dominant grunt and began moving in his direction. The moment Greg saw the buck, he realized by the deer's body language that the animal was very relaxed and at ease. The buck resembled a big, confident wrestler walking around the ring before a bout. Greg was able to easily draw his bow and make a good, clean killing shot. This beautiful buck had a basic ten-point frame with forked brow tines, which made a total of twelve points, and weighed 310 pounds live weight.

It's critical to understand which distinct call will motivate a buck when you are formulating a calling sequence.

Greg Hood with the massive buck that answered his call.

White-tailed deer make many vocalizations: buck grunts, doe grunts, yearling grunts, and spotted yearling bleats. There are several different variations to these vocalizations, which reflect contented, aggressive, and dominant behavior. Whitetails do not vocalize as much or as loud as most hunters believe. A radical bowhunter must understand that to be successful in calling, you have to add passion to your calling technique—not more calling.

Preston always tells me an old saying that if a turkey could smell, you would never be able to kill him. That's exactly what a mature whitetail buck is—a turkey that can smell. That is why they are the hardest big-game animals to harvest. As a hunter, you must understand this right up front if you are going to be able to get a shot at one with your bow. As in turkey hunting, you need to be completely concealed, including wearing a full face mask and gloves. It is also very important to wear a Scent-Lok suit to eliminate your human odors.

And believe it or not, a turkey call sometimes can be a perfect tool to help you bag a big buck. This technique will work better on private land, if only for the safety issue. As you move toward your treestand, pull out a turkey call and put it to work—especially if you bump out a deer or two on your way. Preston is the one who invented this tactic, and it works extremely well during the early bowhunting season. Use clucks, purrs, and very soft *kee-kee* sounds, because they fit perfectly with the time of year. Add realism by scratching the leaves around on the forest floor with your feet, and occasionally make the soft barks of a squirrel. If a buck doesn't wind you, you may be able to sneak right up on top of him without his being even slightly aware of your presence. When the deer hear the sounds of a turkey, they assume that it's safe to go to that area. Because turkeys and deer usually feed on the same types of food, the deer think they can dine out in that area as well.

Once you're in your stand, don't use your deer call too often. It will sound unnatural to the deer, and they will spook out of your shooting range. Use a twenty- to thirty-minute break after your calling, and vary the volume. Team up with a buddy and simulate a group of deer calling back and forth to each other. This will encourage a buck to investigate to see what is happening.

If you are having a difficult time getting within bow range of a buck, are putting the sneak on from the ground, or have a buck moving past your stand location too quickly, try a snort call. In most cases, this will stop a buck dead in his tracks, but he will be on his highest alert, so be ready to take the shot.

The moment you start using your deer call, the buck will be able to pinpoint the exact location where the sound originated. On his approach, he will use his senses of sight, smell, and hearing to pick you out. In most cases, you will be unaware of his exact location, but he knows where you are from the calls you made. At this point, the buck has become the hunter, and you have become the hunted. So keep your cool and wait for the prospective shot. When the opportunity presents itself, take it. Do not wait for a better chance, because most times it will never come.

TIPS FOR CALLING DEER WITHIN SHOOTING RANGE

- Calling will be effective only if you match your tactics and overall strategy with the behavior of the bucks at the proper time of the hunting season.
- The best calling responses from bucks will always be around the rut's peak period. Blow loud, choppy putt grunts every twenty to thirty minutes using random five- to ten-second sequences. Bucks will respond by coming to you, thinking another buck is in the area trailing a doe.
- During the postrut period, tone down your calling and set up very close to a bedding area or a funnel that leads to a primary food

Once you are on stand, be patient and don't call too often. It will sound unnatural, causing the deer to move off safely out of bow range. JOHN DZIZA

source. The bucks are worn out from the rigors of the rut, and they will not travel very far out of their way to check out the calling source.

- Use aggressive calling by grunting more frequently and louder. Let's face it, this could be a long shot, but the insistent calling could bring a good buck right to your location.
- Try grunting at every buck you see that is working away from you out of bow range. What do you have to lose? Most times they will at least stop and look in the direction of the call.

CHAPTER 18

Using Scents to Shrink the Playing Field

A radical bowhunter uses scent to attract big bucks, thereby shrinking the playing field. A white-tailed deer is a scent-oriented animal. Its sense of smell is its strongest and only independent means of protection. If a deer hears something strange in the woods, it will stay and continue to investigate until it can decide whether to take flight; if a deer catches a whiff of something or someone foreign, however, it immediately bolts to safety. Anyone who is serious about bagging a good buck but is hunting without the use of scents is not taking advantage of an important tool for counteracting the impressive powers of a deer's nose.

Those who advocate the use of scents and find success using them probably do so because they are serious bowhunters. In other words radical bowhunters who use scent properly are those who take the time to properly prepare for a hunt—their use of scent is just one more tool they employ as part of their overall hunting strategy.

My good friend Ron Bice of Wildlife Research Products and I have spent decades studying and using every different kind of scent available to attract white-tailed deer. Over these years we have made a lot of mistakes, but we learned from every one of them. We have had rewarding results in recent years using the knowledge we gained. Depending on scenting conditions, which change constantly, we have bowhunted using scents from the extreme northern reaches of the whitetail range to the Deep South, hunting big bucks with consistently successful results. Our success rate with scents is roughly 95 percent—that is, about 95 percent of the time we've bagged a big buck. Now think about the success rate at an average bowhunting camp. If a group of ten was bowhunting in an average scenario, you'd probably expect two bowhunters to take mature bucks—a 20 percent success rate. That's quite a difference. It seems important, then, that every aspiring radical bowhunter be armed with as much knowledge about scents as possible.

The first step in mastering scent is very basic, and it starts with you. The hunter's greatest enemy is perspiration. It is imperative that a bowhunter take every precaution to eliminate human odor from reaching the keen nose of the whitetail buck. Everything starts with human scent elimination, as the time and situation will allow. You need to keep your own scent in mind, and take steps to minimize it, no matter whether you are on a seven-day pack-in adventure to Alaska or hunting your own back forty with all the modern conveniences of home.

Cleanliness is the first step. Ideally, before hunting day, you should have all your clothing washed and charged up and stored in a Scent-Lok storage container. Good old-fashioned clean for your clothing—and for you as well. Avoid using perfumed or strong smelling soaps, aftershave, or cologne. Even mouthwash can give you away. A deer's nose is probably 100 times sharper than man's so you must take every precaution to eliminate body odor. Wash thoroughly. There are products available like the "Scent Killer" line from Wildlife Research Center that can be used for your personal ablutions as well as laundry. Shower just prior to the hunt. Spray your hands with Scent Killer before getting dressed and again after getting into your stand.

The purpose of all this cleanliness is to reduce the amount of human odor molecules that drift from your body to the white-tailed deer. By doing this successfully a radical bowhunter won't trigger a buck's inner alarm. Think about the amount of smoke it takes to trigger a smoke alarm in your home. This will be relative to the amount it would take a white-tailed deer to go on full alert, and turn inside out. The smoke detector is gathering all these molecules out of the air, but nothing happens until suddenly one more molecule and it's over the limit and the alarm goes off, screaming a warning to the inhabitants—loud enough to wake someone who sleeps as I do, like the dead! Remember also, a white-tailed deer can discern a human presence without running off, just as we can tolerate a level of unpleasant skunk odor before we relocate. Deer will tolerate a certain amount of human scent before they bolt.

When using scent remember the number-one rule: absolutely nothing disguises all human odor! Be extremely careful when walking to your hunting area, setting up a mock scrape, or laying a trail of scent to attract deer. Don't move or bend or break branches with your bare hands; use rubber gloves. Using gloves will enable you to make your preparations without leaving tell-tale scent from your hands on everything you have touched on your way into and out of your stand location.

Many bowhunters only think of today's hunt—but how about tomorrow and the next day? Consider all the human scent you are leaving behind in the deer woods; it can stay and alert deer for days. That's why you have to take every precaution to eliminate as much human scent as possible. I've been at this for many years and I've learned that you will never totally eliminate human scent, but you have to do the best you possibly can and consider every scent-related detail. Think about every action you're planning thoroughly, step by step, before taking it, factoring in the scent-creating possibilities. Following this process, and taking steps to minimize your human odor in the woods, might pay huge dividends in the future.

For many years I raised, trained, hunted, and judged beagles and big-game hounds in competition. It didn't take me long to realize how well these hounds smell the scent of the game they were put on to track. I have put a good cold-nosed dog on the two-day-old track of a black bear or mountain loin, and he would in most cases be able to straighten the tracks out and get a good chase going.

A white-tailed deer smells as well as a dog; so keep that in mind the next time you are leaving your human scent all over the home range of the buck you are attempting to bowhunt. Scent lingers sometimes for days.

Always wear proper footgear. Rubber boots are best because the leather type can let your perspiration pass through the sides of your boots and onto the brush as you walk through the woods. If you cannot wear rubber boots at least use the rubber-bottomed kind, or your scent will leach into the ground with each step.

Any human excretion—saliva, urine, or perspiration—will be detected and wave a red flag. Don't contaminate the area; any human odor will alert and spook the deer.

You can use a scent to cover up human odor or as a sexual attractant. You may also combine their use and effectiveness by using both a masking scent eliminator for you and a lure for them. Used this way, the scents become a two-pronged tactic. To use scents properly, they should be a part of your total hunting scheme. There are no shortcuts or guarantees. Do your scouting; knowledge of the terrain, trails, scrapes, and bedding and feeding areas is important to capitalize on the use of any scent.

More bowhunters use scent incorrectly than any other hunting tool. There are two things many bowhunters fail to do properly when using an attractant scent that affect their overall success with these products. The biggest mistake is contamination of the scent setup with human odor. When you are using these products, you must think like a trapper and use the same precautions they do when setting up a trap. Even the most

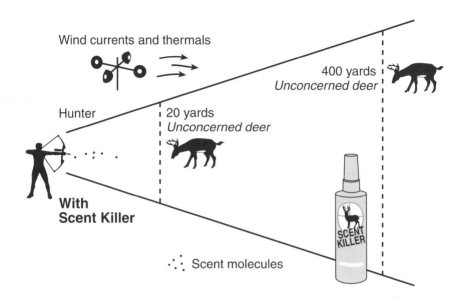

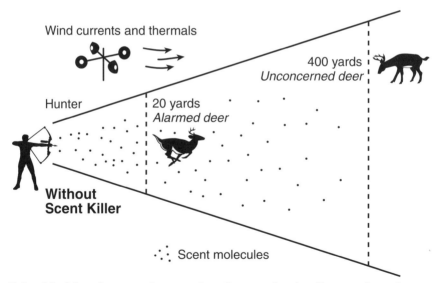

It is critical for a hunter to be scent-free. Scent molecules disperse through wind currents and thermals. WILDLIFE RESEARCH CENTER

interested whitetail buck out there will show hesitation if he believes the hot doe has a predator ready to pounce on or attack her. The other major blunder is to not fully understand the various types of scents and to use them in the wrong situations.

TYPES OF SCENTS AND WHEN TO USE THEM

Following are the different types of scents, and why they work, and when to use them.

- **Territorial scents.** Urine and musk secretions generally from the same kind of animal you are hunting. They work similarly to when a dog urinates on a tree or fire hydrant and another dog comes along, smells it, and urinates over the first dog's marking. When a whitetail detects another buck's scent, he considers it the sign of an intruder.
- **Hunger scents.** Food smells that arouse the whitetail's appetite.
- **Curiosity scents.** Smells that appeal to a white-tailed deer, such as Trails End 307, which has been the top-selling curiosity lure for the past twenty years.
- **Sexual attractants.** Urine collected from does while they are in estrus. Freshness and the collection process are the keys to how well these products work. These are the number-one scent products purchased by bowhunters.
- **Cover (or masking) scents.** Strong natural odors derived from plants or animals that are used to cover up human scent.

Knowing when during the hunting season to use these different types of scents is critical to your success. Here's a suggested scent calendar.

- During the early season, starting in late August and continuing into early September, use a hunger or curiosity lure.
- During the prerut—in October in the North but later in the South— and up to two weeks before the peak of the rut, add a territorial lure to your bag of tricks. One I find effective for the prerut phase is Mega-Tarsal Plus. Few lures bring in the bucks with greater regularity than a good territorial-intrusion scent.
- Once you see the bucks actively seeking out does during daylight hours, it's time to introduce sexual attractants, which will be most effective as the rut reaches its peak. Wildlife Research Products Special Golden Estrus has been consistently effective for me over the years.

Wear rubber gloves and boots to avoid contamination of attractant lure. Use the correct lure for the time of the season. WILDLIFE RESEARCH CENTER

Pro-Wick setup diagram

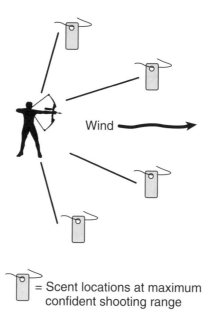

Wind ➝

= Scent locations at maximum confident shooting range

Make sure you are using the right attractant lure for the time of the season you are hunting. WILDLIFE RESEARCH CENTER

- After the rut, you can use all four types of scents with positive results until the end of the hunting season.

DISPENSING SCENT

One of the best ways to dispense scent is with a Pro-Wick setup. This product is much more absorbent and convenient than the old method of film canisters with cotton balls, making it far superior. It is packaged to remain scent-free, but you still need to wear gloves. Put several drops of your preferred scent on the wick, then hang it about five feet off the ground to the left of your stand location, at your maximum confident shooting range. Do the same off to your right. Then place a couple more wicks out in front of your location. The advantage of this setup is twofold: When a buck comes by, he'll intercept this scent before your human scent, and the scent will bring him into range, giving you an opportunity for a good shot.

Another method for dispensing scent effectively is by laying a scent trail. Place scent on an applicator tied to a string. Drag it behind you and off to the side on the way in to your location, leaving a scent trail.

Single stand trail pattern

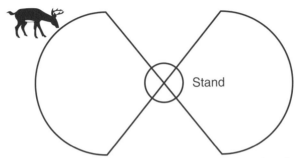

Leave a scent trail from your treestand or ground-blind location that will effectively attract a buck. WILDLIFE RESEARCH CENTER

Dual stand connecting scent trail

A double dose of scent on a scent trail will be doubly effective if you are buddy hunting. Mr. Big is sure to pass one ambush site or the other.
WILDLIFE RESEARCH CENTER

Refreshing your drag with scent every hundred yards or so will keep the scent strong all the way to your stand.

A multidirectional scent trail is another effective way to entice a deer. When a buck encounters a man-made scent trail, it's anybody's guess which direction he will follow it. Take the guesswork out of it by making loop trails so it won't matter which way he goes. Start a scent trail at your stand location. Lay the trail by walking a big loop off to one side of the stand. Make another loop off the other side of the stand. This creates a figure-eight pattern with the stand in the middle. No matter which way the buck follows his nose, he'll be brought right past your stand.

A hunter-to-hunter setup can work extremely well when you are bowhunting with a buddy. Two hunters walk to the same stand. Once there, one hunter heads to the other stand, laying a scent trail all the way. When a buck cuts the scent trail, it doesn't matter which direction he

Mock scrapes set up close to a bedding area can produce buck activity during daylight hours. Make the most of your entire hunting day.
WILDLIFE RESEARCH CENTER

decides to follow. Either way, he'll be headed right toward one of the waiting hunters.

COVER SCENTS

Cover scents, or masking scents, are another type of scent with a different function: preventing the deer from detecting human scent. The use of cover scents along with human scent elimination products can go a long way toward a successful hunt. They work by blending a strong natural scent, generally one native to the hunting area, with our human odor. Some of the better-known cover scents are red fox or raccoon urine and various plant derivatives.

Use the appropriate cover scent for the situation you are hunting. I like to use high-quality fox urine on my boot pads to help cover my trail going in to my stand. More than once, I've seen a fox come slipping through during a deer drive. Seconds later, deer came busting through on the exact same trail as the fox. Deer have a high regard for the fox's nose and seem to feel safe when they encounter the scent. Raccoon urine is an excellent masking scent for treestand bowhunters, as these animals climb trees. You also can match the cover scent to the tree where you have your treestand hung. If it's an oak, try acorn scent; if it's a pine, try cedar. For a ground blind in a cornfield, use corn scent on the outside of the blind.

Select a tree of the same species that bucks in the area are using for scraping activity to make your mock scrape under. JOHN DZIZA

MOCK SCRAPES

The use of mock scrapes is another effective tool for a radical bowhunter. The goal of a mock scrape is that it quickly becomes an active one. Your mock scrape should be placed under a tree as close to the bedding area as possible without impacting the area for morning and evening hunts. The advantage of making them in these locations is that it gives the buck more security to work the scrape outside his bedding area, and he feels safe there. In addition, you should see the most daylight activity in these areas. The closer you get to an open feeding area, the less daylight scrape activity there will be, if any. The only time you should hunt the area is when you can get in and out without being detected.

It is important to select a tree of the same kind that the deer use in your area for their natural scrapes. If they set up under an apple tree, use an apple tree for mock scraping. The tree needs to have an overhanging branch that is approximately the same height from the ground as the deer

Use an overhanging branch that is approximately the same distance from the ground as those found at a natural scrape. This will lend your man-made scrape realism.

WILDLIFE RESEARCH CENTER

use for their scrapes; the average is about four and a half feet in most areas. Cut off the overhanging branch from a tree of the same species over an actual scrape near a feeding area. Attach it to the branch overhanging the scrape you are creating so it drips right on the overhanging branch. Next, hang an Ultimate Scrape Dripper about a foot above the overhanging branch. This will give you an instant active scrape. Remove all the debris from the ground under a tree with a large stick until you have freshened the earth in a twenty-four- to thirty-six-inch circle. Size does matter, because you also want the visual effect; you want the buck to be able to see it. Basically, you are creating a trap for the deer, and you will be set up and waiting in ambush.

The type of attractant lure you should use in the Ultimate Scrape Dripper depends on what time during the season you are creating your mock scrape. During the early season, use a territorial scent such as Select Doe Urine. As the prerut starts, switch to Mega-Tarsal Plus, which is a

Never kneel on the ground to create a mock scrape; your scent will be transferred, thus contaminating the scrape. Instead, use a long stick or branch to clear debris and dig up soil. JOHN DZIZA

Look at the size of this mock scrape turned active. Several bucks have torn up the ground in a four-foot circle. WILDLIFE RESEARCH CENTER

dominant buck scent, and use this until two weeks before the peak of breeding activity. At this time, introduce Special Golden Estrus into the dripper. Even though scrape activity is next to zero during the peak breeding time, continue using the lure in the dripper throughout the remainder of the deer season. Those big bruiser bucks will come back to these scrapes after the breeding cycle ends, and there will be action until the second rut period.

Keeping human scent to a minimum while incorporating these simple-to-use methods will greatly increase your odds of success in the deer woods. Always wear rubber gloves and boots when making a mock scrape, and never kneel on the ground.

TIPS FOR USING SCENTS

- It all starts with you. Practice personal cleanliness from head to toe. Use only scent-free equipment and clothes.
- Make scent use part of a total strategic plan. It's not the magic bullet but an integral part of an overall plan.

- Take precautions to keep your scent pure and effective. Keep it cool and out of direct sunlight. Store any unused portion in the refrigerator.
- Use a scent eliminator to mask your entry into the woods, along with rubber gloves and boots to avoid leaving unwanted human odor where you walk.
- Cover scents can help you remain undetected in the woods. Make sure you use one that is native to your area.

PART FIVE

HOW:

Hunt successfully with truly radical advanced tactics

CHAPTER 19

Sometimes the Best Stand Is a Blind

There is no more exciting way to hunt a monster buck than from a ground blind, where you are at eye level with your opponent. The ground blind also offers numerous advantages, including the ability to hunt in bad weather, move without being detected, and bowhunt in places without trees on which to mount a stand. Some of my most memorable bucks were felled from a ground blind . . .

Every sunrise casts a magical spell on me, and that early-October morning was no different from any other. It was about ten minutes into shooting light, and I caught a glimpse of movement to my right. Out of the bottom walked a monster buck. I could see the breath steaming out of his nostrils as he slowly walked toward my ground blind. The light-colored antlers he sported looked enormous, even though he had body proportions of awesome size.

He held his head down slightly as he slowly and cautiously approached me. I could tell by his body language that he was the boss buck on this turf. He didn't walk; he swaggered. He was a proud, old boy.

My heart was pounding so loudly that it blocked out all other sounds. He was almost within range and needed to take just a few more steps to enter my comfort zone, or the killing zone of twenty-five yards.

Drawing my bow to full draw, I anchored and picked a spot. I took a deep breath, held it, and squeezed my release. The next thing I heard was the thump of the hit. Then I watched, fascinated, as the arrow disappeared through his ribs. It was a perfect

Had I not abandoned my treestand and moved to a ground blind, I would not have bagged this impressive 248-pound monster that scored 163 inches. JOHN DZIZA

hit. The old brute bolted for the cover of some nearby standing corn and vanished from my view. To say I was excited is a gross understatement. Barely able to control myself, I used every ounce of self-discipline I could muster, sat back in my seat, and thought about what had brought me to this time and place . . .

Hunting in Iowa was love at first trip, and after five years, I had tried a new wrinkle in my hunting strategy: I decided to go out for the season opening in the beginning of October. I was playing a hunch that the big guys would be very comfortable, as no hunting pressure had been exerted yet. I was hopeful that they would still be in their early-season patterns.

This would enable me to pattern them, predict their movements, and set an ambush plan in a minimal amount of time. Such a strategy would let me concentrate on the actual hunting phase of the trip.

It was much warmer than I expected on arrival. Almost 80-degree weather made it feel like summer, not whitetail-hunting weather. The deer were not moving much during the heat of the day, and the activity was at first light and just before dark. Much of the foliage was still on the trees, as leaf drop had not gotten into full swing yet. The heavy foliage obstructed my view and also would affect the distance of any potential shot, unless I could get a shot on the edge of a field.

I had sighted a really big buck from my treestand on the second morning, but he was 184 yards away, according to my range finder. On the fourth night, just before dark, I watched the same awesome buck pick his way from the edge of a cornfield back into the bottom. That was twice that I had seen the same buck go in and out at the same spot. It was apparently an ideal way for him to travel, as deer take the path of least resistance. It also represented the shortest distance in the open as he darted into the corn. The bottom rolled up to a point on the edge of the cornfield. The edges had high grass and little sapling trees that gave him just enough cover as he surveyed the field to make sure it was safe to cross.

Unfortunately for me, this route presented a big problem. There was nowhere for me to erect my treestand along that point, and putting my stand back in the timber would leave me guessing which actual travel route the buck would be using on any given day. It wasn't a pretty picture.

I had most always hunted from above, but now that this scenario presented itself, I felt as if I had to switch strategies. I had a plan. The next morning while in my treestand, I very carefully checked out the area with my binoculars as I tried to decide where to put up a ground blind. My eyes kept going back to that cornfield. It was the best place to set up.

I knew that a strategy is a critical part of any hunt, especially for bowhunters. We usually associate hunting strategy with finding the perfect spots to hang our treestands. But there are some situations and places in which it is smarter to abandon the advantage of elevation in order to get closer to a good buck. This buck I was chasing preferred the environment of the cornfield over that of the woodlands; another buck may prefer a swamp. In such cases, a ground blind may be a better option.

ADVANTAGES OF GROUND BLINDS

Why would a radical bowhunter choose a ground blind over a treestand? Ground blinds have many positive features that give them an edge over traditional treestands:

Ground blinds can be more comfortable in very cold or inclement weather, allowing you to sit longer as you wait for a big buck. JOHN DZIZA

- *Carrying and setup.* Portable blinds are much lighter weight and quieter than a treestand and can be set up in a matter of a few seconds.
- *Comfort.* You can be more comfortable in a ground blind because you can use the chair of your choice inside it.
- *Visibility.* Your movements are better hidden from the sharp eyes of deer.
- *Noise.* Blinds muffle noise more than do treestands.
- *Scent.* Enclosed blinds minimize human scent more than open treestands.
- *Safety.* Elevated treestands can be dangerous. Every year, deer hunters are permanently injured or even killed as a result of falls from treestands.
- *Weather protection.* A blind keeps you more comfortable in cold or inclement weather. If it's cold and wet outside, you may become chilled to the bone in a treestand and bail out by 9 A.M. A big buck could show up at 9:30, and you'd miss the opportunity you waited for all season.

- *Multiple hunters.* You can use a blind with a family member or friend, letting you share the bowhunting experience with them by your side.
- *Young hunters.* Using a blind may be just the ticket when introducing a youngster to the sport. My son enjoys hunting with me but finds sitting still very difficult. A blind allows him some freedom of movement without blowing his chances at a buck.
- *Excitement.* Perhaps the most enticing reason is more emotional: Being at eye level is much more exciting than hunting from a treestand. You are right up close and personal.

WHERE TO SET UP

As a progressing radical bowhunter, your scouting should reveal where a buck is feeding and bedding and where his major travel lanes are located. If the buck you have been scouting suddenly seems to disappear, don't give up. Sometimes a buck that is happy and secure in the hardwoods throughout the summer and early autumn abandons the area when the leaves drop and he feels exposed. Stop and think: Where is that buck likely to go?

If it is a mature buck that has been educated by several years of encountering hunters in treestands, he'll go where he feels safest. He may remove himself from pressure by retreating to a swamp, a stand of softwoods, or an area with new-growth hardwoods where the trees are too slender to support a treestand but offer cover dense enough to provide security. That's what my guy did. Depending on the local topography and how close the area you are hunting is to agricultural areas, the buck may instinctively move into a cornfield or other cropfield, which can provide him with both safety and food.

When a buck picks out his bedding areas, he tries to take advantage of the wind, the lay of the land, and anything else that will allow him to feel safe or enable him to survey the area while resting. A buck will instinctively seek out a high spot in a field of corn that enables him to gaze about below him as he beds down. Each rise can provide a vantage point for a reclining deer.

Often a large, old oak tree stands silhouetted against the sky, with short grasses growing around the base that will make a great private bed for a buck to curl up on while he surveys the field. This is not the spot for a treestand, but it's a great example of a good situation for a ground blind. With a ground blind, you can set up close to the bedding area without disturbing the deer, as you would if you tried to reach the tree in order to set up a treestand. Clumps of thick brush in swampy areas can

Setting up a ground blind in an area where a buck is forced to cross an open spot can be a very productive tactic for a radical bowhunter. JOHN DZIZA

also be good places to set up a ground blind. Use this tactic if you know that a buck will be returning to his swampland bedroom after a night on the prowl.

If a big buck can best be ambushed from a ground blind, there are several things a radical bowhunter can do that will help set up a shot. First of all, it is very important for the bowhunter to disappear into the surroundings, but the camouflage pattern you use in your treestand will not always work for ground-blind hunting. Just think about the surrounding environment. If you are going to search out your super buck in a field of dry corn, a tan camouflage pattern may work better than one that is predominantly green. You can use the same camouflage patterns that you use in a fall goose field in these situations; they'll blend in very well.

KINDS OF GROUND BLINDS

You can opt to set up a temporary ground blind fashioned out of natural materials, buy a roll of material in one of several different camouflage patterns with which to construct your own blind, or purchase one of the excellent manufactured portable ground blinds available today. Whatever you choose to use, your blind has to blend in to your surroundings, and it is critical to eliminate silhouettes, especially in an open area.

I always have at least one portable ground blind in my bag of tricks anywhere I go, even if I have to ship it to my destination before I arrive. You never know what is going to happen. I'd rather tote one and not need it than wind up empty-handed at the end of my hunt. Sometimes I do come up empty, but I try to stack the deck in my favor.

SUCCESS

As with any type of hunting, technique has a lot to do with success or lack thereof. So on that warm October afternoon, I put my plan in place for this big buck. I carefully set up my Double Bull ground blind at the end of the cornfield. When I stood back to admire my handiwork, I couldn't believe how well it actually blended in. It was almost invisible, but I knew it was there. Now all I had to do was wait it out and hope that the buck would cross in this natural funnel and enable me to blind-side him.

Over the next few days, a number of deer passed by my blind, and I could have almost reached out and touched them. I knew then that this was a very effective setup, because I was still seeing deer. The wind seemed to favor me from my angle, but I was taking no chances with odor detection and was wearing Scent-Lok protection, a classic liner with a camouflage system on top. The wait continued.

Finally it was getting down to the wire. It was my ninth day hunting, and I had scheduled a ten-day hunt. Soon I would have to return home. I settled in at the ground blind early in the morning and waited for shooting light. It was a spectacular morning, and my hopes were high. And that's when I finally got my chance at that big buck . . .

As I waited to retrieve my buck, I realized that I had been daydreaming about how I came to be here and glanced at my watch to check the time. I had been woolgathering longer than I thought, and it was time to leave the ground blind and find my buck. I walked along the edge of the corn and there, forty yards away, was a fantastic buck. The closer I got, the larger his body looked. His rack was shining in the morning sunlight, and it too looked massive. When I reached him and lifted up his head, I marveled at the twelve points his antlers sported.

I was even more amazed at the sheer bulk of him. I felt a real sense of accomplishment, especially considering that I'd been hunting outside my normal time preference, which is usually just prior to the peak of the rut. It had also culminated in taking a good buck, using a method different from most bowhunters. It was an exhilarating and unique hunt.

The buck green-scored 163 inches and weighed 248 pounds dressed. If I hadn't used the ground blind, I firmly believe that I never would have had an opportunity at this magnificent buck.

This ground blind is practically invisible; it blends right into the cornfield. JOHN DZIZA

CHAPTER 20

Don't Shoot a Small Buck If You Want to Bag a Big One

If you really want to bag a big buck, do not shoot any other deer in that area. During my many years of studying the behavioral habits of the white-tailed deer herd after harvesting a good buck—or any buck—I have observed that the event will totally upset the social structure of the deer herd in the area for up to a week. What this means is if you—or anyone—shoots a buck, the entire herd will lie low. Furthermore, mature bucks will be the last to return to their normal patterns. If you know that big buck is there, wait for him to show himself. If you take a small buck out, you may never get an opportunity at Mr. Big that season.

Being able to exert this type of discipline may depend on how much time you have to hunt an area. Many hunters just do not have unlimited amounts of hunting time. (Isn't it incredible how things like a job can really bite into hunting season?) Sometimes any buck is better than no buck at all—or is it?

True radical bowhunters always pass on the lesser bucks and wait for that one chosen exceptional buck—because by doing so, they become trophy hunters. What makes a usually sane person, appreciative of creature comforts, leave a warm bed in the dark of the night to sit aloft and alone in frigid temperatures? What has him or her holding on to a bow instead of a pillow, for hours and hours, only to pass up an easy shot at a good buck in the hopes of an opportunity at a bigger or better one? Only a radical bowhunter can answer that question. For only a radical bowhunter has evolved to the state where easy is not good enough. Only a radical bowhunter can say why waiting for a specific individual whitetail buck becomes the basis of how the hunt is played to its climax.

The radical bowhunter . . . the words conjure up all types of images, depending on who hears them. Antihunters would have everyone envision a rich and self-indulgent type who pays big bucks for exotic big game

Shooting an immature buck will upset the social structure of the herd.

This two-and-a-half-year-old will mature into a dandy buck in a few years. Notice that his rack is still between his ears. JOHN DZIZA

Learning how to field-judge a buck on the hoof will help you develop into a radical bowhunter. Let the small one go so he can grow. JOHN DZIZA

Although this buck may look like a shooter, neither his body nor his antlers have fully developed. His legs are long, and his body has the lean look of an athlete from back to belly. A radical bowhunter would see the potential and wait for him to achieve his full glory.

in fascinating places, such as on an African safari. This theoretical trophy hunter would be ruthless and callous and interested in what they perceive as the slaughtering of animals to feed his own ego. Yet this vision is wrong. A novice bowhunter would think of a mentor who has had experience in the field and can temper the excitement of seeing a buck by letting a lesser or immature one pass to grow into a more experienced adversary. The radical bowhunter may see himself or herself as an avid and intense bowhunter who is committed to the love of hunting on a higher plane. It is this passion for bowhunting that makes a radical bowhunter, not merely the desire for a monster rack to hang on the wall.

The legacy of bowhunting has been handed down from time immemorial. Man always has been a predator. Antihunters feel that because society has shifted from a rural setting, where people were dependent on and close to the land and what it produced for survival, to an urban setting where food is easily obtained at the grocery store, hunting for food

If you shoot a little buck, you will not get the opportunity at a big one. Be patient and be discriminating.

is undesirable. But wait—they think that anyone hunting at all for any reason is undesirable. So much for what they think. I think that I enjoy bowhunting and pursue my pleasure in hunting every day, whether or not I am in the woods. Every day, I am reading, talking, or reminiscing about, or preparing for or returning from, a hunting experience. Do I eat, drink, and sleep hunting? Almost.

In hunting, I find that the tension and stress of my daily existence seem to fall away as I contemplate nature in a very personal way. That level is intensified to an all-encompassing degree of concentration by singling out an individual buck to hunt—my "trophy," as it were. I have committed myself and my attention to zeroing in on one individual buck that I will match head-to-head in the time-honored challenge of the hunt.

I will try to get to know everything I can about this individual: where he eats, sleeps, and roams, and how the terrain and weather affect his movements. If I can, I'll use the lay of the land to try to find just the right spot for our confrontation. A mature whitetail buck is a wily creature. Many times, I wind up the season without claiming a good buck. But all in all, the season is still a success, for after all, that buck is out there waiting for me to pick up the challenge again next year.

CHAPTER 21

If It's Light Out, Hunt!

Everyone knows that dawn and dusk are great hunting times, but a radical bowhunter knows that big bucks can be active all day long. I have seen—and documented in my hunting logs—many instances of mature bucks on the move during midday hours. Several factors may influence this movement, and serious hunters should understand and be able to take advantage of all of them. There are three primary situations that stimulate midday big-buck movement and demand that radical bowhunters be in their stands from dawn to dusk:

- *When there are high levels of hunting pressure from other hunters in the area.* Hunter activity will completely disrupt deer behavior, leading to unusual movement patterns. Because hunters are in their tree-stands in the morning and evening, it follows that deer might move in full daylight at midday if they sense that other hunters have departed the area at this time.
- *During the peak of the rut.* At this stage of the season, deer can be moving at any time of the day, rather than only during the typical hours of dawn and dusk. Dominant bucks will be focused on one primary activity—chasing hot does all day long. They don't stop for lunch at noon like most hunters!
- *During extreme weather conditions.* Inclement weather provides exceptional opportunities for bagging a trophy, but also exceptional challenges.

Radical bowhunters use the weather to their advantage and meet the challenges of extreme weather. Cold weather is one of the most important factors stimulating midday buck activity. During very cold weather, the temperature is often warmest at midday. Whitetails need to eat more to

This buck was taken at 1:15 P.M. on a late-December bowhunt. They really do move about at midday.

stay warm, and limiting movement to the warmest part of the day helps them conserve energy. By not exposing their body to extremely cold temperatures, they can minimize the loss of body heat resulting from radiational cooling.

Of course, conditions that affect deer will also affect hunters. During severely cold hunting days, many hunters cannot stay on stand for the entire day. Unfortunately, too many leave their stands around midday for lunch or simply to warm up, not realizing that this is the time bucks will be moving about. Bucks are wise to the comings and goings of hunters and can tell when the lunch whistle blows. When they hear (or see or smell) a hunter leave their territory, they will then venture forth to feed.

I have hunted Saskatchewan for many years during our Thanksgiving week. (I wonder if my wife is giving thanks that I am hunting again? That leaves her free to shop on the busiest shopping day of the year. What a trade-off!) Without fail, when the temperatures get extremely cold, the

My friend Bob Bain shot this impressive buck at high noon during Connecticut's peak of the rut.

majority of buck movement during the day is between the hours of 10 A.M. and 2 P.M. I actually pray for 20-degree-below-zero temperatures! Buck activity is stimulated by does. Does move during this time because it is the warmest part of the day and they use less energy getting food. The big bucks move at this time because the rut is in full swing and they are following the does.

Bowhunting in these extreme conditions is more than difficult; it can be downright dangerous. Over the years, I have seen many a hunter come up north thinking they are prepared for the hunt in these conditions, but after a few hours in a treestand, they are so cold they have to bail out and go back to camp. They spent all that money to hunt, but their hunt is ruined because they have inappropriate gear and are unable to hunt in those conditions.

Bowhunting in extremely frigid temperatures actually starts before you get dressed in the morning. First, you must eat a good breakfast that is packed with plenty of carbohydrates to help you stay warm. This is particularly important for treestand hunters, because they are elevated and exposed to the wind and weather. Pack a few peanut butter and jelly sandwiches in your Scent-Lok backpack to stoke your metabolic furnace during the day. Carbohydrates help your body generate heat as your system digests the food.

Next, select appropriate clothing. Insulation reduces heat loss from your body, and it is very important to wear a layering system with a well-insulated hat and boots. The hat is especially important, because you will lose a large amount of body heat through your head; in cold weather, a bare head is the quickest route to a cold body. The whole body radiates heat, but when you get cold, your system reduces circulation to your extremities, especially feet and hands, to help maintain the blood supply to the head. Because of this, your feet will feel cold if they are not protected properly.

Sitting on a heat-generating insulated foam pad can be an effective way of reducing contact heat loss, but you might need to turn to technology for an advantage over big bucks on extremely cold days. The EZ Series Heater Body Suit, a whole-body insulating system, is one such product; it should be an essential part of your gear when you want to hunt the entire day in bone-chilling weather. This suit allows you to wear lighter clothing, which enables you to shoot the bow much easier than if you were wearing heavy, bulky clothes and boots. The suit has internal shoulder straps that allow it to slowly and quietly slip off your shoulders and out of the way of your bow. Let's face it—if you aren't warm, you either fidget or leave the woods entirely. And if you can't shoot your bow properly because of bulky clothing, you could miss a shot at the big buck of your dreams. Wearing too much clothing as you walk in to your hunting location will cause you to sweat, and after you're in the treestand for a few hours, you'll be freezing to death.

Once you've outfitted yourself for the conditions, there is one more essential key to success: You have to be in your hunting spot when the buck comes by, or it's impossible to kill him. Now that sounds like a silly thing to have to say, but most bowhunters hunt only what they consider the peak times, which are the first few hours of daylight and the last few hours of legal shooting light. Some have good intentions but just don't stick it out all day long from dark to dark. It's extremely difficult even when the weather cooperates, but when it's exceptionally cold, with gusty winds and snow or rain, sitting out there in the deer woods can be a test of your discipline and mettle.

Covering your head and hands not only reduces heat loss on a frigid day, but also eliminates your human odor if you use Scent-Lok gear. JOHN DZIZA

Wearing an EZ Series heater body suit enables a bowhunter to withstand frigid temperatures while on stand all day. JOHN DZIZA

This awesome buck was caught on film at 1:37 P.M. He was probably waiting for a hunter to go to lunch. A radical bowhunter will sit on stand all day long for a buck like this. WILDLIFE RESEARCH CENTER

Consider a scenario with two bowhunters of equal ability. One has only a week to hunt but has every fancy new hunting aid on the market, while the other doesn't have any gadgets but has lots of time to bowhunt—the entire season if he needs it to get his buck. Who do you think has the best odds of scoring? I'd put my money on the hunter with all the time, before the one with all the bowhunting aids. Let's face it, the basic foundation for bowhunting trophy whitetail bucks successfully is time on stand combined with discipline and a planned-out strategy. The bottom line is that a radical bowhunter will hunt whenever and wherever possible. I guarantee that if you spend enough time out there, you will put your tag on many more big bucks than all your friends do. There have been times over the years when, if I had looked out the window and gone back to bed, I never would have shot that buck that day, or perhaps not any day. Remember, you can't kill a buck if you're sitting back at home.

Several years ago, we had a blizzard on opening day of our deer season. It snowed heavily all night, and by early morning, we had about eighteen inches of snow on the ground and it was still coming down. Thank God for four-wheel-drive pickup trucks, because I would not have gotten out of my drifted-in driveway that morning otherwise. Even the main roads were unplowed and treacherous to travel, despite the four-wheel-drive. Now who else but a radical bowhunter would go out bowhunting in this weather? No one in his right mind would venture forth in this spectacle of nature's fury. But despite the snow over our knees, my two buddies and I saw at least as many deer moving that day as on any other opening day since we had been keeping records, if not more. All the other hunters were back home in bed or shoveling their driveways—which meant virtually no pressure. By the end of the day, I had put a tag on a really nice, heavy eight-pointer that scored 142.

White-tailed deer do not have any set daily agenda or schedule to follow. How often have you seen deer—even a nice mature buck—at times of day and in places you never expected to see one? Several really dedicated white-tailed deer biologists have spent many years studying the animals, trying to solve the puzzle of their behavior with very few answers. A white-tailed deer is a very unpredictable wild animal. So the best thing a radical bowhunter can do is to prepare well and stick it out in the field for as long as possible. Because if you have done your homework, you will eventually see that trophy buck where you hoped to—and then all you'll have to do is shoot straight.

CHAPTER 22

Corn Stalking, Swamp Walking, and Tracking

A radical bowhunter goes where the big bucks are—even if that means delving into huge cornfields or wading through swamps. Let's face it, there are times when the deer just are not moving around during daylight hours. It could be because it's too hot, very windy, or raining heavily—the reason isn't important. At these times, you can just sit there and watch the time go by, or you can employ some active radical tactics in challenging habitats that just might put you on to that big buck.

First, a word on safety is required: No matter how familiar you think you are with a swamp, marsh, cornfield, or other challenging habitat, on a cloudy or rainy day it is very easy to get turned around and lost. Walking around in a thick, dense cedar swamp or a midwestern cornfield, with the tight rows and stalks higher than one's head, even an experienced bowhunter can become confused. Always carry a good compass and map and a GPS unit with you; check them before you enter the area to get your bearings. It's smart to carry some type of fanny or backpack with enough water, food, and gear to get you through a night, in addition to some type of signaling device.

Some of the biggest and most-sought bucks have historically made their homes in swamps and other wetlands, and this is true across the entire range of the white-tailed deer. River bottoms typically have an abundance of different high-quality food sources, helping the bucks that live there grow quickly. The soil is very rich, producing the high-quality food that the deer eat, which in turn enables the bucks to attain tremendous weights and heavy racks. Although many wetlands flood at some time of the year, they usually have several places with dry ground that allow you to hunt throughout the bow season.

Most swamps (which I will use as a generic term for flooded habitat) have some type of creek, stream, or river running through or into them. If so, you can use a small boat or canoe to penetrate the depths of the swamp, getting as deep as needed while hauling your gear in and out quietly. A boat can also come in handy if you harvest a good buck; it will be the easiest way of getting him out of that swamp.

The bucks use trails in a swamp just as they do on dry land. They have certain routes they use consistently when crossing water. Most times the trails they use are related to the depth of the water. Not surprisingly, bucks always seem to cross at the shallowest points in the swamp. If you can pinpoint a few places where the water is the shallowest, you will greatly increase the odds of seeing a good buck. This requires that you scout a swamp throughout the year, especially during drier seasons. When scouting, look for any natural humps or small ridges in the swamp; they will be visible when the water level is low. Even when these areas are covered with water, the bucks know where these high places are and will use them in their travels. Once you find these potential shallow-water locations in a swamp, save them in your GPS unit or mark them on your map. Being able to quickly relocate these spots during the hunting season might help you harvest more bucks.

To successfully hunt swamp bucks, you have to get into the water with them and put up a treestand over the water in a strategic location.

These bucks will bed on high spots in the swamp out of the water. Setting up a treestand close to these beds can be very productive for a morning ambush. Rubs facing the water's edge usually indicate an exit route from the swamp. Hanging a stand in a tree about ten yards into the swamp near the rubs and along the exit route can be very productive.

Even though bucks move almost silently in the water while they feed, in most cases you will hear them long before you see them. On a very still morning, I've heard a buck scoop acorns up off the top of the water and even could hear the water dripping from his mouth as he picked them up. Then I heard the cracking, popping sound of the nuts as he crushed them with his teeth. In a swamp, you can hear for a much greater distance because the water is still and very calm, and there is no vegetation around your treestand to muffle the sound.

Several years ago, I watched an impressive 160-class buck wade into a swamp and look back toward the land a few times. It was at the end of day, with about fifteen minutes of legal shooting light remaining. The buck bedded down right on the edge of the water. He could hear and see anything coming his way from the land from his great vantage point. From my treestand location in the swamp, I spooked the buck out of his bed, back into the water right by my stand, by throwing a rock onto the land near him. As he slowly passed my ambush site, located right off his trail through the swamp water, I drew my bow, picked a spot, and released an arrow. The arrow instantly hit its mark, drilling him through both lungs, and he bolted frantically deeper into the cover of the swamp. I could hear the splashing water as he moved. Suddenly I heard the final splash, and it was over. We had matched wits one-on-one, and this time I was the winner.

A swamp can be a very game-rich area that most bowhunters never penetrate. So here you go, radical bowhunters—a new spot that has not had pressure. When you venture into these areas that are less frequented by hunters, you will likely be entering the home turf of the most mature and biggest bucks in the vicinity, animals that very few hunters ever get to see.

Swamps aren't the only refuge areas whitetails will use for their best defense. White-tailed deer also use standing corn as a safe haven, especially in the Midwest, with its miles upon miles of cornfields, interrupted now and then by a soybean field, then followed by more corn. White-tailed deer are very adaptable and can thrive in fields of standing corn.

Most hunters believe that deer in cornfields are unhuntable until the fields are harvested. Many farmers today leave the corn standing in the fields long into the autumn to allow the crops to dry naturally, saving them the added expense of using propane gas-powered dryers after the grain has been harvested. Furthermore, in seasons with heavy rainfall, the fields become muddy and inaccessible, and the corn has to stay in the fields longer. This means more food and safety for the whitetails inhabiting those fields.

Several years ago, I was bowhunting the early season in southern Iowa. The weather was unseasonably warm, with wind and lots of rain, and the corn was still standing. The deer were not moving during the day because of the conditions, making for extremely long days on stand. The Midwest offers the ultimate in funnel hunting, because once the crops have been harvested, the deer are forced to use the little cover remaining to travel between bedding and feed areas. But when the crops have not been cut and the weather doesn't cooperate, midwestern hunts can be the toughest of all—if you don't use some radical bowhunter tactics.

You actually can use standing corn to your advantage in seasons when the crops are still standing. Most bowhunters I've spoken with are stymied by a deer's tendency to hole up in cornfields, and they wonder how the animals can even survive in the corn. They can't seem to figure out how to hunt a buck from a treestand or ground blind on the edge of a typical cornfield that is a square mile in size.

Make a radical move—go deep into the woods to find your buck. Packing into the woods and camping for a few days can give you the edge you need.

White-tailed deer—especially bucks—feel safe and secure in a cornfield because it provides them with everything they need to survive—cover and food and water—and they rarely scent or see a hunter. Bowhunters can use standing corn to their advantage by stalking right up on top of the animals in the cornfield without the deer having a clue they are there. Did you ever listen to the crackling and rustling of unpicked corn in the slightest breeze, as the leaves and husks rub against each other? As long as the air is moving at all, the deer will never hear you, because all the sounds the corn makes will cover most noises you make as you slip through the field.

Slowly walk each cornrow with the wind in your face. Poke your head through the stalks carefully, looking to the left and right down each row for a deer that could be hiding in the corn. Even if a deer does see you, he will be so surprised that he will often freeze long enough for you to get off a quick shot, so always be on the alert and ready. It's truly amazing how close you can get to a deer by slowly and quietly moving when you are completely camouflaged from head to toe. This tactic demands exceptional patience and skill to get within shooting range, but once you have taken your first buck in a standing cornfield, you will have accomplished something that most bowhunters have never even thought to try.

Hunters seem to never want to leave their treestands, and in many parts of the country, still hunting in the woods is truly a lost art. To be able to slip within reasonable distance of a monster buck demands woodsmanship, a skill that most hunters cannot—or will not—invest the time to acquire. Bowhunters who are careful observers, and who refuse to be distracted by the unrelated sounds of the woods, will see plenty of deer as they slowly and deliberately follow the track of a buck. Big-woods deer have much larger home ranges and are harder to pattern, but they still have the same traits as any other whitetail. Most good big-woods bucks are taken each year by trackers who pick up the track of a good buck and follow it until they find him, usually bedded down.

Probably the most famous trackers are my good friends the Benoits from Vermont. These guys are experts at getting on the track of a big buck and tracking him down like bloodhounds. You don't have to possess the skills of this famous family to be successful, but the more comfortable you are hunting away from the nearest road and escaping the sounds and signs of humanity, the more successful you'll be. The key is that you must be totally focused and alert at all times because, depending on the cover, a big buck could be right under your feet at the next step, especially in fresh, powdery snow.

Always be alert when tracking a buck in fresh snow. Stop, look, and listen.

Slowly and deliberately follow each track, and use a quality pair of binoculars to search the cover ahead, looking for parts of the deer. Most times you'll never see the entire animal, only small parts of him. Bowhunters must train their eyes to look for such things as the white inside an ear, an eye, antlers (they are not moving branches), or the white and black around the tail. Work a zigzag pattern that heads in the direction of the tracks; on a still hunt that's done correctly, your forward progress as the crow flies is very slow. There is no real reason to rush if you are in a good area, because you know the bucks are there. The goal is to find them before they find you.

CHAPTER 23

The Radical Bowhunter's Arsenal: Don't Cut Corners on Your Equipment

A *Sports Illustrated* columnist recently wrote about all the gadgets hunters employ. He was mocking us, asking if we really needed all those technological advantages just to kill a deer.

Obviously, we do not. In fact, if any one of those toys made it so much easier, I wouldn't use them. I'm reminded of the uproar in the 1970s when depth finders hit the fishing world. People claimed fishermen would fish out the lakes. Then in the 1990s, when underwater cameras were introduced, the naysayers were up in arms, pronouncing the end of fishing as we know it. Once again, that didn't happen.

The same is the case with many of the innovations in deer hunting. They are tools that enhance our enjoyment of the experience. Yes, they give us a slight additional advantage, but the last time I checked, there were still plenty of deer. In fact, there are more deer—and more big deer—now than ever before.

Deer hunting is recreation. If it were too easy, if the challenge were gone, we'd quit doing it. But the fact is, more people are bowhunting than ever before.

Every year, I do lots of seminars on hunting deer. People always ask me questions after I am done. The vast majority of these questions pertain to my equipment—the tools in my big-buck hunting arsenal. The weekend hunters all want to know what radical bowhunters use to increase the odds and enhance their enjoyment. So here goes . . .

BOWS

Certainly the most important piece of equipment for a bowhunter is the bow. In my early days of bowhunting, I used a recurve. I'd spend countless hours practicing just to become proficient at a very modest distance. My goal was to be able to hit a paper plate every time at twenty yards. Then, and only then, would I feel comfortable taking to the woods. I'd shoot most of the summer so that come opening day, I was completely capable of making the right shot.

The early compound bows offered the mechanical advantage of let-off. The let-offs in those days were maybe 40 percent, not the 80 percent of today's bows. But being able to hold at full draw to aim was a big improvement. Those were two-cam bows, however, and they never really were perfectly tuned, so I still shot all summer long in order to be proficient.

One of the greatest innovations in bowhunting was the invention of the single-cam bow—and not just because single-cam bows offer tremendous accuracy advantages. The inherent stability provided by the single-cam system led to myriad other advantages, including less noise, recoil, weight, and length. Less is definitely more in a bow.

I have been shooting a Mathews bow since shortly after they were first introduced in the early 1990s. As a Mathews pro staffer, I have the opportunity to shoot the latest model each year. The thing that truly blows me away is how each year's model is notably better than the previous. I still love to shoot all year round, but I no longer have to tinker with my bow to get it to shoot. It takes me no time at all to get my new Mathews shooting darts, or I can just pick up my bow from last year and start shooting.

Confidence is at the core of athletic prowess. It's not hard to be confident when you're shooting the best bow ever. Do you need a really expensive bow? No. But my philosophy has always been to buy the best equipment available. Quality products outlast inferior products, and they don't fail in the field. I know my days of worrying about bow problems while in the backwoods are over.

ARROWS

The right arrows can make a big difference, too. The biggest issue here is to make sure your arrows match your setup. Too many people assume that any kind of arrow will perform. Buy name-brand arrows, and have your pro shop verify that the spine and length are appropriate for you and your bow. My experience is that good arrows are more consistent than cheap arrows.

I go to the trouble of marking each arrow with a code number. You'd be amazed how often it's the same arrow that's flying wild. There's nothing like an occasional flyer to create doubt in your mind about your abilities. Remember, confidence is key. Don't let a lousy arrow mess with your mind.

Carbon or graphite arrows offer significant speed advantages over aluminum arrows. And though I am not a speed freak—today's bows shoot an arrow so much faster than the bows of yesteryear anyhow—a faster arrow means a flatter trajectory, which gives you an edge when judging distance. A flatter trajectory means more room for error. I've been shooting the new cross-weave Carbon Express Maxima, and for me, they shoot the best out of my Mathews bow. They are the strongest 100 percent carbon arrows available. I just returned from northern Manitoba, where I drove one of these arrows completely through a six-foot, eight-inch black bear, breaking ribs on both sides of this big bruin. Later, I was able to wash off the arrow and put it right back into my quiver!

I store my arrows in a Mathews ArrowWeb quiver. A quiver is a prime cause of noise, which is a key reason for misplaced shots, but this model is quiet. I absolutely love the ability to adjust the gripper to hold different-diameter arrows. I use this feature to clamp down my arrows so they absolutely cannot vibrate.

I'm always amazed how many weekend warriors shoot without their quivers attached to their bows during practice and then wonder why their arrows don't fly perfectly in the field with the quiver attached. You need to practice with your quiver attached, because it adds a little weight and alters the balance of the bow.

BOWSIGHTS

I use a Black Gold FlashPoint bowsight. It's rugged, simple, easy to adjust, and reliable. I never have a problem with it. Like any well-made product fashioned from superior materials, it costs a bit more but I do not like to have issues while hunting.

One of its features is a round pin guard, which I like to line up in my peep sight. The truth of the matter is that my bow can shoot inside a nickel; it's me that's the problem. If I can at least make sure I'm lined up in the same way every time, my chances of shooting well are dramatically improved.

ARROW RESTS

One of the biggest frustrations the weekend bowhunter has is broadhead flight. A great innovation to address this issue is the fall-away arrow rest, which holds your arrow in position until you release the bowstring, at which time the rest falls out of the way. The key here is arrow contact. With a traditional arrow rest, your arrow rides the rest until it leaves the bow. Any hand torque you apply to the bow is transferred to the arrow. And more important, your fletchings or vanes can contact the rest as the arrow leaves the bow, which can certainly affect the flight as well.

Because a fall-away rest falls away, you have less time to apply any hand torque, and the fletchings or vanes simply do not touch the rest. The result is better shooting accuracy, especially with broadheads, where any error is magnified. When bowhunters ask me for help with their shooting, the first thing I suggest is getting a single-cam bow with a fall-away rest.

I use a FreeFall fall-away rest, the only one that uses an internal mechanism to activate the fall-away process. As you've already gathered, I do not like potential problems. An inertia-activated fall-away rest eliminates the need for external connectors to engage the fall-away process.

BROADHEADS

Broadheads have certainly evolved in recent years. A big debate in the last decade has been over fixed-blade versus expandable broadheads. Fixed-blades have been around for a long time and are proven. Expandables offer the advantage of less profile for reduced planing. The trade-off is possible deflection once the arrow penetrates the animal. With the new Rage expandable broadhead featuring the revolutionary SlipCam Rear Blade Deployment System, you have three big advantages:

1. Eliminates deflection. An angled hit with an over-the-top expandable can result in the leading blade grabbing first and throwing the head off-line. Rage's rear deploying blades follow the cut-on-impact tip and will not grab or deflect.
2. Guarnateed fully deployed blades. High-speed footage of over-the-top heads shows the blades do not fully open until they enter. Rage's rear deploying blades are guaranteed to be fully deployed before they enter, which means you'll get the benefit of the heads' full-cutting diameter.
3. No loss of kinetic energy. Rage's expandables eliminate deflection and are fully deployed upon entry, which means no loss of kinetic energy and superior penetration. Talk about the best of both worlds.

TARGETS

A disadvantage of such innovative equipment is the fact that one no longer has to shoot so much to become a proficient archer. But fortunately, because it is so much fun, most bowhunters still do. A key reason that it's fun is that today's targets are so much better. I used to visit local farmers to buy hay bales, which I would stack in the backyard to shoot into. Then, as it got cold, I'd use them to cover my wife's roses. When the first 3-D targets came out, I'd practice shooting at the "real thing" from a treestand in my backyard. Boy, have things changed . . .

Layered targets have made the old targets obsolete. The Block was the first layered target, and it continues to lead the way. I have a Block in my yard and shoot broadheads into it all year long. As the shafts slip in between the layers, the heat and friction stop arrows quickly. And because there is no puncturing, the targets last a long time.

The same foam layers have since been incorporated into a 3-D target called the GlenDel Buck. Now I can shoot at a realistic-looking deer and have the easy arrow-removal advantage of layering. Why is this so important? Well, if you've ever wrestled with other types of targets, you know it gets tiresome. These targets let me enjoy shooting without the hassles. I have no doubt that by minimizing target-practice hassles, these targets have increased the likelihood of a clean shot significantly.

Especially for newer bowhunters, it's important to shoot from all the positions you might encounter afield. Hunters tend to practice standing erect, shooting at a target at eye level in the backyard. When is the last time you shot a deer while standing erect at eye level? You need to practice from a treestand, shooting all the angles, even behind you. Practice from your blind while sitting, kneeling, and crouching. Practice with the same heavy clothing you will surely be wearing when it's cold outside in the late fall. Practice to make the first shot count, not the last. A radical bowhunter is prepared for any shooting situation that comes up.

THE STANDS

I spend a lot of time hunting around the country and sometimes have to hunt from other people's stands, and my number-one priority is safety. I prefer to hunt from a ladder stand. It's easy to climb into, and I never have to rely on the integrity of a branch while climbing. Climbing stands are useful in certain parts of the country where pole-style trees are the rule. Hang-on stands are the most popular, in my opinion, because they are lightweight, making them easy to carry, and cheaper. Rivers Edge makes all the treestands I use when I am home. Make certain you understand how your treestand works and are comfortable with it before you head out on opening day.

The most important safety device is your safety harness. First, let me say this: Do not hunt from an elevated position without a safety harness.

Hunting without being connected is just plain stupid. Also, do not affix a stand without a safety device. I will walk back to my truck to grab my harness before I hunt without it.

The most exciting product I've seen in years is the Fall Guy Treestand Restraint System. Designed by automotive safety engineers out of Detroit, it lets you stay connected to your tree from the time you arrive—while climbing up to your stand, while hunting, and while climbing down—all with a retractable strap that attaches to a special vest. It works the same as the seat belt in your vehicle. If you start to fall, centrifugal force and a fly-wheel effect stop the fall immediately. Fall Guy products can save your life. Don't hunt without them. I don't.

GROUND BLINDS

Mark my word: The next revolution in bowhunting for deer will be the ground blind. Hunting from a blind has several advantages over hunting from a treestand. First, it's easier; no climbing is necessary. Second, your scent is held inside the blind. Third, you can move without being detected, which is crucial when that big buck is at twenty yards. Fourth, you'll hunt longer because a blind is more comfortable.

I hunt from a Double Bull Matrix 360. Double Bull is the premium blind builder, and the owners are both fanatical bowhunters. The Matrix 360 has a special window system called SurroundSight, which allows you to see all the way around you. The window system can be easily and silently moved up or down at will, and you shoot through a special camo mesh that conceals you even with the window open.

Talk about exciting. There is something about a big, old buck standing a few steps away from you at eye level. If you've never hunted from a blind for deer, you must try it!

A few tips on blind hunting. First, bring a chair, preferably a stable, three-legged one made for shooting from a blind. Second, practice shoot-ing from your blind through the mesh. It's a confidence thing. Third, make sure you have bright fiber-optic pins on your bowsight. The last minutes of legal shooting time in a blind are pretty dark. Fourth, don't forget to de-scent your blind. I leave mine out in the woods for several days to de-scent, and then transport it in plastic bags. Fifth, make your blind part of the terrain, camouflaging it with brush. Sixth, don't buy a cheap blind. They flap in the wind and the material is too shiny.

CLOTHING AND SHOES

I am a stickler for well-made hunting clothing. When you spend a lot of time wearing it in various conditions, anything less than the best simply will not do. I wear clothing from Gamehide and Scent-Lok. Gamehide is

This monster Saskatchewan buck dressed at 265 pounds and was harvested out of a Double Bull Blind at -30° F.

known for hunting-wear innovation. The fabrics they use are second to none, and the features are obviously developed by hunters for hunters. Scent-Lok is the company that started the carbon clothing craze. The ability to detect human scent is a big whitetail buck's first line of defense, and by incorporating absorptive carbon into their clothing, Scent-Lok has helped me avoid detection by numerous big bucks.

Cold or sore feet can make a hunter antsy and downright uncomfortable. When my "dogs are barking," I am miserable. Thorlos has the most extensive line of sports-specific socks in the marketplace. Think of your feet before you go hunting, because foot pain is preventable. Thorlos has proven it with scientific and medical research. My feet really do feel better since I've been wearing them, and even the coldest temperatures do not affect them. They stay warm and dry in any hunting situation, and I can perform better, longer, and safer when wearing Thorlos. Once you try them, you'll experience the difference that warm, dry, comfortable feet can make when performance is critical.

SCOUTING CAMERAS

Perhaps my favorite new tool is the scouting camera, not just because it helps me find or pattern a big buck, but also because it lets me hunt all year long. My cameras are out twenty-four hours a day, 365 days a year. I also use them while hunting on the road. I put them out to see what happens at stands I do not hunt.

The world of scouting cameras has really changed with the advent of digital technology. The leader is this world is Cuddeback, whose camera was designed specifically for scouting use. Other companies employ off-the-shelf digital cameras that trigger slowly and use up batteries quickly. Once again, performance is worth paying for, and the best scouting camera is Cuddeback. One of my favorite toys is the video clip mode in a Cuddeback. It's fun to see a digital image, but it's even better to watch a video clip.

FOOD PLOTS

One of the biggest changes in deer hunting over the past decades was the introduction of food plots. Once deer hunters recognized that antler growth could be influenced with the introduction of optimal amounts of protein into a buck's diet, we started planting Imperial Whitetail Clover from the Whitetail Institute. Who would have believed that a bag of seed would help us grow bigger bucks on our property?

That then led to the discovery that by strategically placing our food plots, we could alter the deer's behavior. Deer love clover, so they are more likely to come out in the daylight for a gourmet meal.

Food plots have since been augmented by mineral supplements, some of which also enhance antler growth.

A radical bowhunter uses all the tools available to tilt the odds in his favor and make the hunt more fun. A radical bowhunter will not, however, use means that turn hunting into a farce. Always hunt ethically and keep in mind that you're doing this for fun!

CHAPTER 24

A Radical Success Story

This radical bowhunter pays the price to get the big buck, even if it means hunting the same deer for a total of three trips from Massachusetts to Iowa and twenty-three days in the field. Now you have to admit, this sounds like a truly radical story. Here is how it started—and ended with a really nice buck . . .

Out of the corner of my eye, I caught a glimpse of him heading my way through the cover that edged the cut cornfield I was hunting. This was my twenty-third day and my third trip hunting in this spot, this season. Although I'd had opportunities at several smaller bucks, this was my third sighting of this big buck. I had been waiting for this particular buck, which had been captured early in the season by a DeerCam scouting camera that was positioned along his rub line right through this natural funnel.

Picking up my binoculars, I found him in my enhanced view. This was definitely the buck I had been hunting. I was positive. He had a very distinctive set of antlers, with thirteen points and forked brow tines on each side. He had made a very obvious scrape and rub line through this funnel area, and several large trees sported lots of bark damage, victims of his vigorous rubbing. Several of the scrapes along the field edge were being renewed every few days. This was a hot area and I had a new setup, and I hoped he would pass within shooting range this time.

This rub was made on the edge of an agricultural field by the buck I found so elusive.

He was sixty-two yards away, according to my range finder, but he was starting to move. Unfortunately, it was in the wrong direction, and if he continued on that course, he would never pass within range. So I picked up my deer call, put it to my lips, and made three short putt grunts. He instantly stopped and turned in my direction. He was staring again at the decoy that I had set up in the area I wanted him to pass through.

Painstakingly, he began picking his way toward me. Step by step, he got closer and closer, and as in the old commercial, the closer he got, the better he looked. I could see the breath steaming out of his nostrils as he slowly walked in my direction. Keeping my mounting excitement in check was difficult, but I struggled to maintain control so I would not miss an opportunity to shoot if he presented me with one.

He held his head down slightly as he approached. He was the boss on this turf—I could tell by his body language and gait. He was a proud, old boy.

These magnificent monsters are what dreams are made of, and now I had one almost within shooting range. I forced myself to wait until I was sure he was close enough for a good shot. He passed my stand at just twenty yards, almost exactly where I expected he would come. The wind was across my back, and he had never gotten a whiff of my scent because of the great scent-eliminating capability of my Scent-Lok suit. The excitement and pressure were fantastic. I could scarcely breathe. Suddenly I grew incredibly calm and told myself he was within range. Then I waited for him to take two more steps to present a good shot.

He picked up his feet and took the first step that would bring him that little bit closer to my arrow and me. Then another step, and he stopped as if on cue as he looked ahead at the decoy.

Drawing my bow to full draw, I anchored and picked a spot. I took a deep breath, held it, and released my arrow. I heard the familiar *thunk* as the white shaft and feathers disappeared through both his lungs. He bolted and headed directly for the open field. He ran over a little rise about sixty-five yards from my stand and vanished from view. My heart was really in high gear now; I was trembling from the surge of excitement. I had to sit down for a few minutes. While I sat, I started thinking about what had brought me to this treestand in southern Iowa . . .

This little pocket of Iowa is my favorite place to bowhunt big bucks. I am obsessed by big whitetails and have been since I was a kid. I'm always on the prowl for new and exciting places to hunt monster bucks.

A few years ago, I stumbled upon the state of Iowa. Some of my friends thought I was crazy—that is, until I dropped the hunting stats on the table. Iowa has been open to nonresident hunting for just about fifteen years, and it is number one in North America for total entries in the Boone and Crockett Record Book and is responsible for five of the top ten whitetail bucks in the Pope and Young Record Book. Also, Iowa boasts ten of the top forty whitetails (top twenty typical and top twenty nontypical) ever harvested in North America with a bow and arrow, as recorded in Pope and Young. That is a staggering 25 percent of the biggest bucks in the world, and six of them have been harvested since 1993. Those statistics are hard to beat.

Looking deeper, one sees that five of the top ten, nine of the top twenty, and seven individual bucks that score over 190 points are all from Iowa, and that is considering only the animals in the

Pope and Young Record Book. No other state or Canadian province even comes close to these amazing figures.

Considering these numbers, it's probably easy to see why I enjoy hunting Iowa. But nothing is ever easy, especially whitetail hunting. There are drawbacks to every sure thing, and one is Iowa's lottery system. Licenses are available to nonresidents on a draw system. Many potential hunters and guides and outfitters are not happy with that situation, because they earn their livelihood from hunting clients. But on the other hand, that system is what keeps the hunting so fantastic. The number of hunters is strictly controlled, and that ensures that the herd does not get overpressured. Also, the firearm and muzzleloader seasons are after the rut, which saves a lot of those lovesick bucks that are chasing does during that time.

Conducting research to find a general location that holds trophy bucks is just the first stage in becoming a radical bowhunter. After I realized that Iowa was where I wanted to be, I needed to fine-tune my search for an actual parcel or area where I felt I would have the best opportunity to get a chance at a huge buck. I was looking for a large enough parcel that could be managed properly. I knew that many small tracts were available to be leased for hunting. Such areas may be fine, but it's hard to manage them, because you can't control the boundaries from hunters using adjacent plots.

Several years ago, I found a location that contained more than ten thousand acres in one large tract. Much of the land was in (CRP), and the crops were planted for the wildlife, mainly deer, turkeys, pheasants, ducks, and geese. Hunting in Iowa was love at first trip on that plot, and after ten years, I tried a new wrinkle in my hunting strategy. I decided to go out for the season opener at the beginning of October. I was playing a hunch that the big guys would be very comfortable. Because no hunting pressure had been exerted yet, they would still be in their early-season patterns and in bachelor groups. This would enable me to pattern them, predict their movements, and set an ambush plan in a minimal amount of time so that I could concentrate on the actual hunting phase of my trip.

Four days of almost 80-degree weather had me thinking of summer, not whitetail-hunting weather. The deer were not moving much during the heat of the day, and all activity was at first light and just before dark. By the end of the week, I had seen only one buck in the 130 class. I went home empty-handed and planned my next trip. My dream hunting season would be to spend the entire season here and not hunt anywhere else. That is a fantasy for sure, as my writing assignment work tends to interfere with my ideas and dreams.

I learned a long time ago that if you want to kill big bucks, you must go where big bucks flourish. That's the only way we hunters have a realistic opportunity at harvesting one of them. Geographically, this area is a hunting paradise, because the harvesting of the crops causes the ultimate funnel hunt. The bucks in their travel patterns use the little woodlots as they move from one feed area to another in search of hot does during the rut. The key is to find a staging area where the bucks feel comfortable enough to congregate. You will know you have found one by the number of rubs and scrapes you encounter on the perimeters of these woodlots.

On my second visit, I arrived at the end of October and stayed into the first few days of November. By the time a few days had passed, I had seen quite a few bucks, but only two were in the 140 class.

Thursday evening was slow in the stand; I sat praying to catch a glimpse of that heavy-racked buck. I saw a few does. Then *wow,* what a buck! I could see his rack clearly even with my naked eyes, though he was more than three hundred yards away. I reached for my glasses to get a better view. He was with five does and was keeping track of one like a quarter horse chasing a calf.

This buck was the heavy-racked monster with the forked brow tines on both sides that I had been after. I glassed this marvelous 170-class buck for more than twenty minutes with my binoculars, and even though I never got a shot opportunity, it was a great thrill just to watch that magnificent buck work his harem. The following morning, I had to return home again without a deer. But I was trying to figure out how I could get back for a while to continue this hunt in between my other planned trips for the balance of the fall season.

My third leg of the trip began the day after Thanksgiving. Now all I had to do was wait it out and hope that the buck would cross in this natural funnel.

I had watched this buck pick his way from the edge of a cornfield back into a bottom twice. I had seen him go in and out at the

The infamous twenty-three-day Iowa buck. Persistence does pay . . . big time!

same spot during my last two trips here this year. It was apparently an ideal way for him to travel, as deer take the path of least resistance. The bottom rolled up to a point of timber on the edge of the cornfield. The edges were all high grass and open hardwoods. They gave him just enough cover, as he surveyed the field, to make sure it was safe to cross into the heavy cover where he was bedding. It also represented the shortest distance in the open as he darted across during daylight hours. My stand was placed in this funnel, and I felt confident my strategy could work; I just had to wait it out.

The next few days, a number of deer passed by my stand, and I could have almost reached down and touched several of them. I knew then that this was a very effective setup, because I was still seeing deer. The wind seemed to favor me from this angle, and I was taking no chances with odor detection. I was wearing a double layer of Scent-Lok protection: a liner with a camouflage system on top.

Time was running out. I was looking at my twenty-third day of hunting in total from my three visits, and I would have to leave for home the following morning. I tried to take every precaution I could, which included a double shampoo, reactivation of my Scent-Lok clothing, and spraying my bow, binoculars, and other gear with Scent Killer odor eliminator. I was as ready as I ever would be.

I arrived early the next morning. Extra early. I settled in my tree-stand and was waiting for shooting light. I was hopeful but a bit apprehensive. I knew today would be my last attempt at baking this guy this season . . .

I finally realized that I had been daydreaming about how I got here and glanced at my watch to check the time. I climbed down and walked along the edge of the cornfield. As I came over the rise, just beyond it lay the magnificent monster buck. The closer I approached, the heavier his rack appeared. I focused on the tremendous rack, grabbed an antler that my hand could not completely encircle, and pulled his head up for a closer look. This buck was a behemoth, with a tremendous set of thirteen-point antlers and a massive body.

The buck green-scored 172$^1/8$, and he was my third really good buck in four years of hunting in Iowa. Perhaps you can see why I'm obsessed not only with whitetail bucks, but also with this little honey hole.

I felt a real sense of accomplishment, especially considering that this hunt had spanned from prerut to postrut. Great hunts and memories are measured by the effort you put in. I will remember this hunt forever, because for me that's how true memories are made. You can bet I'll be back again next fall for an opportunity to see another bruiser up close and personal. That's what its all about for this radical bowhunter.

Final Thoughts

Many people—bowhunters, gun hunters, even nonhunters—often ask me why I continue to hunt if it is so easy. Where is the challenge? Do I ever miss a buck? Do I ever come home empty-handed? Why will I pass up a lesser buck and thus not take any buck?

It seems my lecture circuit is the catalyst for many questions. Some are technical and may be answered with a piece of advice. Some are more philosophical and are asked by those who may share my sport but not my true feelings about being a radical bowhunter. So for them, and for you, I'll try to sum up what my bowhunting experiences mean to me in hopes of sharing with you not only my expertise, but my viewpoint as well.

Yes, I do pass up bucks over the course of my hunting year. But so do most hunters, as well as fishermen who practice catch-and-release. A novice hunter might, in his excitement, bag the first deer he sees. But as his proficiency increases, he may not be satisfied with a small spike. He may decide to let one pass and wait to see if something a little bigger may cross his path. Ahh—here are sown the seeds of the radical bowhunter, a hunter whose prowess and expertise have allowed him to become discriminating, and whose intense commitments to the sport and pure love of bowhunting have enabled him to reach a different plane of hunting. It's not much different from any other sport or hobby. Once an aficionado has been immersed in the interest and has obtained some basic knowledge and experience, he seeks a higher level of participation than he was able to enjoy as a mere beginner.

Bowhunting is what it's all about for me. It's sharing a legacy passed on by older generations. I am a bowhunter. I am a trophy hunter. I am a *radical bowhunter.* I pursue this sport because it is an integral part of my life that I enjoy like nothing else. It is a lifelong avocation that offers me experiences that supersede the actual trophy.

For although a big buck is a fundamental part of the experience, the real trophy is the appreciation of the solitude and the calming, quiet effect this experience has on my harried day-to-day existence. There are times when that serenity is more than enough and the trophy is spiritual, something that will beckon me another day. And when you reach this place, you will understand that you have evolved into a true radical bowhunter.

Resources

Black Gold Premium Bowsights
FreeFall Rests
25-B Shawnee Way
Bozeman, MT 59715
(406) 586-1117
www.montanablackgold.com

Faster trigger speed,
longer battery life

Cuddeback Digital Camera
DeerCam
Non Typical, Inc.
860 Park Lane
Park Falls, WI 54552
(715) 762-2260
www.cuddebackdigital.com

The Makers of Premium Hunting Blinds

Double Bull Archery LLC
301 County Rd. 43
Big Lake, MN 55309
(888) 464-0409
www.doublebullarchery.com

Field Logic, Inc.
101 Main St.
Superior, WI 54880
(715) 395-9955
www.fieldlogic.com

Gamehide Hunting Wear
CORE Resources, Inc.
1503 E. Highway 13
Burnsville, MN 55337
(888) 267-3591
www.gamehide.com

Martin Archery
3134 W. Highway 12
Walla Walla, WA 99362
(509) 529-2554
www.martinarchery.com

Mathews, Inc.
919 River Rd.
P.O. Box 367
Sparta, WI 54656
(608) 269-2728
www.mathewsinc.com

North Country Whitetails
(315) 331-6959
www.northcountrywhitetails.com

Quality Deer Management
Association
(800) 209-3337
www.qdma.com

Rivers Edge Treestands
Ardisam, Inc.
1360 First Ave.
P.O. Box 666
Cumberland, WI 54829
(800) 345-6007
www.ardisam.com

Scent-Lok Technologies
1731 Wierengo Dr.
Muskegon, MI 49442
(800) 315-5799
www.scentlok.com

Whitetail Institute of North America
239 Whitetail Trail
Pintlala, AL 36043
(800) 688-3030
www.whitetailinstitute.com

Wildlife Research Center
1050 McKinley St.
Anoka, MN 55303
(800) 873-5873
www.wildlife.com

Zebra Strings
919 River Rd.
P.O. Box 367
Sparta, WI 54656
(608) 269-1235
www.zebrastrings.com

Index